Withdrawn

Cook it!

Cook it!

THE DR. SEUSS COOKBOOK FOR KID CHEFS

BY **Daniel Gercke**

PHOTOGRAPHS BY CHRISTOPHER TESTANI

RANDOM HOUSE
NEW YORK

Visit us on the Web!
Seussville.com
rhcbooks.com

Educators and librarians, for a variety
of teaching tools, visit us at
RHTeachersLibrarians.com

Design by Jennifer K. Beal Davis

ISBN 978-0-525-57959-5

MANUFACTURED IN CHINA

10 9 8 7 6 5 4 3 2 1

First Edition

For Lolz
—DG

Contents

PART 3
Oh, the Dishes You'll Cook 103

From there to here,
from here to there,
YUMMY things
are everywhere.

Dr. Seuss in Your Kitchen

HAVE YOU EVER WANTED TO TRY GREEN EGGS AND HAM?

Or feast on Roast Beast? Or sip Pink Ink like a Yink? Of course you have! Did you know you can make them yourself? All you need is a kitchen, a grown-up, a few just-right kitchen tools, and some fresh ingredients. Oh, and the secret ingredient, of course. You've already got it right there, between your ears: the secret ingredient to all Seuss-Food is a heaping handful of IMAGINATION.

Imagination makes food fun! And fun food is much more exciting and tasty than regular food.

In this book there are fifty fun recipes for you to try. You'll frizzle green eggs, beezle a chickpea, trim a Truffula, and whisk with a Wocket. You'll pfoosh and squinch and gloop, and when you're done, you'll feast on food made with the help of your very own imagination.

The recipes are gathered into three parts:

PART 1: BEGINNER SNACKS

The first part has simple, delicious snack recipes where you can take the lead (with a little help from your grown-up), even if you're just starting out as a cook.

PART 2: FUN THAT IS YUMMY

The recipes in the second part take a little bit MORE: more steps, more help from your grown-up, and a bit more kitchen experience under your belt.

PART 3: OH, THE DISHES YOU'LL COOK

The dishes in the third part are the snazziest. They are for cooks who have cooked a lot and are comfortable using many different kitchen tools.

But you'll find at least some jobs that are just right for you in every recipe in this book. Any cook, whether you're a Tot or a Teen or a Somewhere-in-Between, can help make great food by adding imagination and fun.

Because a cook is a cook, no matter how small!

A starting-out cook needs a grown-up or two—
someone to show all the things you can do.
Grown-ups are useful, to have one is good.
Do you have a grown-up for cooking? You should!

Training Your Grown-Up

DO YOU HAVE TO DO ALL THIS ALONE? OF COURSE NOT!

Grown-ups are here to lend a hand. Here are some ways you can train your grown-up to help you with your cooking.

- **Talk with your grown-up about kitchen rules.** Clear cooking rules make confident cooks.

- **Take your grown-up shopping for fresh, wholesome ingredients.** This will make you a better cook, and a healthier one, too.

- **Read through the entire recipe with your grown-up.** That's how you'll know which tools you'll need, which jobs you can do yourself, and which ones you'll need help with.

- **Ask your grown-up to slow down and show you how things are done.** What tools do they use? How do they use them?

- **Make a mess with your grown-up, then clean it up together.** When everyone cleans together till the cleaning is done, the cleaning is more fun.

- **Remind your grown-up it's okay to make mistakes.** There's no better way to learn how to cook.

9 Tricks of the Seussian Kitchen

Here are nine tricks that will help you succeed,
98 and 3/4 percent guaranteed.
These nine little tricks keep your kitchen skills strong.
Follow them all, and you'll never go wrong!

1 Wash your hands well before touching the food.

2 Put on an apron so stains won't intrude.

3 Listen to grown-ups— they know what to do.

4 Read the whole recipe all the way through.

5 Set out your ingredients right at the start.

6 Be careful of hot things and sharp things. Be smart.

7 Clean between steps what is no longer needed.

8 Cook with your senses—all five should be heeded.

9 Be patient, have fun, and do not sweat the spills. The kitchen's the place to try out your new skills!

Kitchen-Things-in-a-Box

Most kitchen cabinets and drawers are full of cooking tools, which come in all shapes and sizes. Which ones will you use in your cooking? That depends on the recipe and what tools you are ready to use.

Always ask before using a tool that is new to you, and give yourself time to learn to use it well. You might even set aside a few kitchen tools that are just right for you to use. The fun ones, the colorful ones, the just-right-for-your-hands ones. Store your special kitchen things in a drawer, box, or container—your very own Kitchen-Things-in-a-Box.

Don't let your Kitchen Things run wild! Make sure to clean your Things well and put them back safely in their box every time you use them.

YOUR THINGS MIGHT INCLUDE:

- Measuring cups and spoons (one set for dry ingredients, one set for wet)

- An apron or a large T-shirt to wear over your clothes

- A wooden spoon

- Oven mitts

- A vegetable peeler

- Clean scissors (used only for cooking)

- Just-right cutting tools (see page 23)

- A rubber spatula

- A cutting board

- A pastry brush

- A whisk or two

Now, boxes of Things
are not only for Cats—
a box could contain
a young chef's this-and-thats!

Sharp things and hot things are needed for cooking
(but don't ever use them when grown-ups aren't looking).

Sharp Things . . .

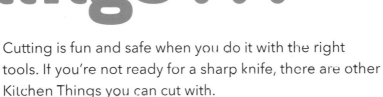

Cutting is fun and safe when you do it with the right tools. If you're not ready for a sharp knife, there are other Kitchen Things you can cut with.

- **A pizza wheel for herbs or greens**
- **Clean scissors (used only for cooking)**
- **A butter knife for spreading, or for slicing soft ingredients**
- **A plastic serrated knife to saw through many foods**
- **The edge of a metal spatula or dough scraper to separate softer ingredients**

Always use a stable cutting board made of wood or plastic when cutting and chopping. (You can place a damp paper towel underneath the board to help keep it from slipping while you work.)

Do you have a grown-up's permission to use a paring knife or a chef's knife? If so, make sure it's sharp. Dull knives are dangerous, because they are hard to use and can slip. When carrying a knife, keep the point toward the floor. Always cut by pushing the knife AWAY from you, not toward you. Ask your grown-up for a lesson.

. . . and Hot Things

Most recipes need to be cooked, and that means using heat. HOT heat, the kind that hurts to touch! Here are some tips for treating heat right:

- **Only use a stove or microwave with your grown-up's permission and help.**

- **Use oven mitts or pot holders for handling hot pans or trays.**

- **When cooking on the stove top, turn pan handles to the side so nobody will knock them over.**

- **Watch out for spattering oil or boiling water from hot pans.**

- **Double-check that the stove is turned off when you're done.**

- **Stay alert in the kitchen and don't get distracted! Hot things can look the same as cool things.**

There are plenty of kitchen tools
just right for YOU,
so don't worry much
if you can't use a few.

SIZZLE
SIZZLE

PART 1

Beginner Snacks

Perfect for little chefs learning to cook,

these snacks are the simplest to do in this book.

The ones that come first can be done the most easily,

but all of them can be made ever-so-breezily!

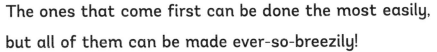

Cat Hat Parfait

CREAMY YOGURT AND HONEY PARFAIT WITH FRESH STRAWBERRIES

Can you layer red fruit and white yogurt to look like the stripes on the Cat's hat? The sweet strawberries and creamy yogurt make this healthy enough for breakfast and yummy enough for dessert!

---

9 tablespoons whole-milk or low-fat plain yogurt

¼ teaspoon vanilla extract, plus more to taste

¾ cup chopped fresh strawberries

1½ teaspoons honey

1. In a bowl, whisk together the yogurt and vanilla. Taste and add more vanilla if it's not vanilla-y enough.

2. To an 8-ounce glass, add 3 heaping tablespoons of strawberries. On top of that, put 3 tablespoons of vanilla yogurt. Then drizzle that with ½ teaspoon of honey.

3. Repeat step 2—berries! yogurt! honey!—two more times until you ALMOST reach the top of your glass. Try to build each layer evenly. Finish it with berries on top. Don't let the parfait overflow!

I know a game, a game that is yummy.
All we need now is some yogurt and honey.
Strawberries help, and a tall, empty glass.
And now let's begin our Striped-Hat-Making class.
We'll build one and eat it in five minutes flat.
You'll see, it's delicious . . . or I'll eat my hat!

Cheese Trees

HOMEMADE CHEDDAR CHEESE DIP WITH CELERY AND BROCCOLI "TREES"

An easy-peasy cheesy dip with crunchy veggies. Measurements don't have to be precise in this recipe, so you can't go wrong. The mushing of the ingredients is a simple, fun job.

4   ounces cream cheese, softened

3   tablespoons sour cream or plain yogurt

¾   cup (3 ounces) shredded sharp cheddar

¼   teaspoon granulated garlic or garlic powder, plus more to taste (optional)

Large pinch of kosher salt, plus more to taste

Dash of paprika

¼   cup minced fresh parsley (optional)

Celery stalks, for serving

Broccoli florets, for serving

1. In a medium bowl, use a potato masher or a fork to mash together the cream cheese, sour cream, cheddar, garlic (if using), salt, and paprika. Mash until mushy. Fold in the parsley, if you're using it. Taste and add more salt and/or garlic.

2. If you like, you can use a vegetable peeler to peel off the fiber-y backs of the celery stalks. Cut the stalks into thirds.

3. Glop the cheese dip into a shallow serving bowl. Serve with celery sticks and broccoli florets on the side for nifty dipping—or stand the celery and broccoli up in the dip to make a Cheese-Tree jungle! The dip will keep for 3 days in the fridge. Just don't freeze it. Freezy Cheese separates when thawed.

Say this three times, sir, and cook to these rhymes, sir: Three free fleas squeezed cheese onto trees. Cheese-squeezing's a breeze, and pleases with ease!

Boxed Gox

GREEN APPLE SLICES WITH ALMOND BUTTER AND RAISINS

This is the simplest of snacks, and one of the tastiest. In one corner, we have: Almond Butter! And in the opposite corner, we have: Raisins! Put them in the box together and *you'll* be the winner. Save any spare cinnamon sugar for future sprinkling. (It's good on Grinch Toast!)

2 tablespoons sugar

2 teaspoons ground cinnamon

1 green apple, cut into quarters and cored

2 tablespoons raisins

2 tablespoons almond, peanut, or other nut butter

1. In a small bowl, mix together the sugar and cinnamon.

2. Cut each apple quarter lengthwise into 4 slices. On a plate, arrange each group of 4 slices so the cut edges on the inside form a box of empty space in the middle of the plate. Sprinkle the apple slices lightly with cinnamon sugar.

3. Pour the raisins into one corner of the box. Dollop the almond butter in the opposite corner. Serve, using the apple slices to scoop the almond butter and raisins.

This is my Gox.
He likes to box.
Apple slices in a square,
a tasty box he loves to share.

33

Hooey Honey Parrot Carrots

HONEYED BABY CARROTS

Even the crabbiest parrot will love these baby carrots, coated in honey and baked until silky. If you have no baby carrots, you can use teenage or grown-up carrots! Just cut them into 1-inch sticks.

1 pound baby carrots, halved lengthwise if thick (or the same amount of regular carrots, cut into 1-inch sticks)

2 tablespoons extra-virgin olive oil

2 tablespoons honey

½ teaspoon kosher salt

¼ teaspoon ground cinnamon

1. Heat the oven to 375°F.

2. On a rimmed baking sheet, toss the carrots with the oil, honey, salt, and cinnamon. Spread the carrots out in an even layer and bake for 15 minutes. Toss and bake for another 25 to 30 minutes, until caramelized and tender. Serve warm.

Said a tongue-tied green parrot named Hooey,
"The stuff on these carrots is gooey!"
But boy did he love 'em.
His beak was full of 'em.
Now Hooey can't talk, they're so chewy.

Do you like Green Eggs and Ham?
You can cook them—here's a plan!
Would you, could you, in a boat?
Would you with a bright green yolk?

Green Eggs and Ham in a Boat

DEVILED EGGS WITH EDAMAME, HAM, AND HERBS

This mellow green version of deviled eggs skips the spicy mustard and perks up the edamame with pink diced ham. If you can't find edamame for your yolks, you'll still be pleased if you substitute peas.

6   large eggs

1   small bunch of fresh basil, leaves only (about 1 packed cup)

¼   cup shelled frozen edamame or green peas (thawed), plus a few more for garnish

2   tablespoons extra-virgin olive oil

2   tablespoons mayonnaise

½   teaspoon freshly squeezed lemon juice, plus more to taste

    Kosher salt and freshly ground black pepper

    Diced cooked ham, for serving

1. Bring a medium pot of water to a boil. Put some ice and water into a bowl next to the stove. Lower the eggs into the pot and boil for 9 minutes. Transfer the eggs with a slotted spoon to the ice water and leave them there until cool enough to handle.

2. Crack the eggs all over by rolling them on the counter (this is the fun part), then peel and cut in half the long way. Transfer the egg yolks to a blender (reserve the whites).

3. To the yolks in the blender, add the basil, edamame, olive oil, mayonnaise, lemon juice, a large pinch of salt, and pepper to taste. Blend until smooth, scraping down the sides of the blender with a spatula. Taste and add more salt and/or lemon juice if needed. Transfer the mixture to a resealable plastic bag, snip off a corner, and pipe into the halved egg whites. Sprinkle with ham and extra edamame. Ready to set sail!

Succulent Succotash Salad

SAUTÉED CORN, LIMA BEANS, AND SWEET PEPPERS

Sweet peppers and corn make this warm salad a swell snack or a superb start to any supper. And succotash is as fun to make as it is to say!

- 2 tablespoons unsalted butter
- 2 tablespoons extra-virgin olive oil, plus more for serving
- 1 sweet onion, diced
  Kosher salt
- 1 red bell pepper, diced
- 2 cups frozen baby lima beans, thawed
- 2 cups frozen corn kernels, thawed
- 3 garlic cloves, thinly sliced
- ⅓ cup chopped fresh basil
- ⅓ cup chopped fresh mint
- ⅓ cup shaved Parmesan, for serving
  Flaky sea salt (optimal), for serving

1. Heat the butter and oil in a large skillet over medium heat. Stir in the onion and ½ teaspoon kosher salt and cook until softened and translucent, about 6 minutes. Stir in the bell pepper, lima beans, corn, garlic, and another ½ teaspoon salt. Cover and cook for 10 minutes, stirring occasionally. Uncover and cook until the lima beans are tender, up to 5 minutes more. Remove from the heat.

2. Stir in the basil and mint. Taste and add more salt if needed. Transfer to a serving plate and top with a drizzle of oil, the shaved Parmesan, and flaky sea salt to taste. Succulent success!

BIG S, little s, what begins with S? Succulent sweet pepper succotash for super salad-y snacks, no less!

TIME: 5 MINUTES * MAKES 2 SERVINGS

Pink Ink Drink à la Yink

FIZZY RASPBERRY SPRITZER WITH LIME JUICE

This thirst-busting, healthy Pink Drink will tickle your fancy *and* your nose! Pouring seltzer over the raspberry purée (the Gloop) is pure fizzy fun. Frozen berries are fine if fresh aren't findable.

- 1 cup fresh or frozen raspberries, plus a few more for garnish
- Juice of 1 lime
- 1 tablespoon sugar or honey (optional)
- 1 1-liter bottle of seltzer water
- Lime slices, for garnish

1. In a blender, purée the raspberries, lime juice, and sugar or honey, if using, until smooth. Press the purée through a fine-mesh sieve into a bowl and throw away the seeds, but keep the purée—this is your Gloop.

2. Fill 2 large glasses with ice. Spoon 2 tablespoons of Gloop into each glass. Top off with seltzer. Stir gently and watch the Gloop change into Pink Ink! Garnish with a few raspberries and a nice slice of lime and enjoy. Gloop (without seltzer) stays fresh for up to 1 week in the refrigerator. Or freeze Gloop in ice cube trays, pop out the frozen cubes, and store in a freezer bag for up to 3 months.

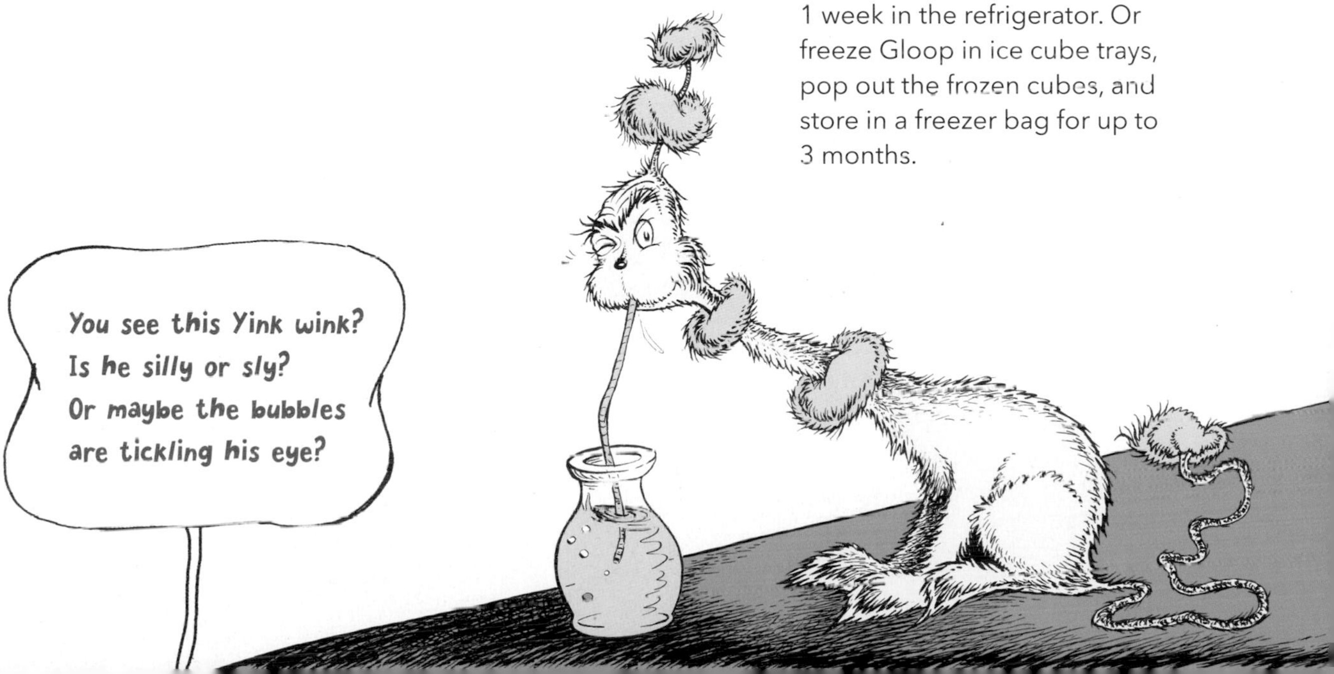

You see this Yink wink?
Is he silly or sly?
Or maybe the bubbles
are tickling his eye?

A Caboodle of Beezle-Nuts

SPICED CRISPY ROASTED CHICKPEAS

Beezle-Nuts are a crunchy snack you can't resist. Just shake them and bake them and gobble them warm. A whole caboodle will vanish in no time!

1 14.5-ounce can of chickpeas, drained and rinsed in a colander

2 tablespoons extra-virgin olive oil

¼ teaspoon fine sea salt

¼ teaspoon smoked paprika (or regular paprika)

Finely grated zest of ½ lime

1. Heat the oven to 400°F. Line a rimmed baking sheet with paper towels and spread the chickpeas over them. Gently pat the chickpeas dry, then throw the paper towels away. (Keep the chickpeas!)

2. On the baking sheet, toss the chickpeas with the oil and salt. Bake until browned and crispy, 30 to 35 minutes, occasionally shaking the baking sheet (carefully!) to move the chickpeas around.

3. Remove from the oven and immediately sprinkle with the paprika and lime zest. Let the chickpeas cool slightly. They are now fully beezled and ready to serve.

A thunderous thunder was shaking the jungle.
Oh! What could make such a tree-shaking rumble?
Well, as anyone knows who has beezled a bunch,
a beezle-nut's taste is as big as its crunch.

Tuttle-Tuttle Crisps

CRUNCHY KALE CHIPS

These healthy salty snacks will perk up even a totally tired turtle. Bet you can't eat just one!

½ large bunch of kale (about 7 ounces)

1 tablespoon extra-virgin olive oil

1½ tablespoons finely grated Parmesan

Large pinch of fine sea salt

1. Arrange the racks in the upper and lower thirds of the oven, and heat the oven to 275°F.

2. Wash and thoroughly dry the kale. (If it's not completely dry, the chips won't crisp up.) Remove the stems and tear the leaves into large pieces.

3. In a large bowl, mix together the oil, Parmesan, and salt. Toss the torn Tuttles (kale) with the oil mixture, using your hands to massage it into

each piece. Divide the Tuttles between 2 rimmed baking sheets, spreading them out evenly.

4. Bake both trays at once until the Tuttles are shrunken and crisp, about 20 minutes. Remove from the oven and allow to cool on the baking sheets. Eat your Tuttles right away (while they're at their crispiest), or store them in an airtight container for up to 1 week.

Ten tired turtles
on a Tuttle-Tuttle tree.
When the Tuttles start to rustle,
then a startled turtle sees
that Tuttles could be tasty
with a bit of salt and cheese.

Gra-Noola

CINNAMON-PECAN GRANOLA CLUSTERS

Oh, these crunchy, nutty gra-noola clusters are perfect to take to all the places you'll go!

Nonstick cooking spray

½ cup maple syrup

½ cup mild honey, such as clover

½ cup neutral oil, such as grapeseed or sunflower

1 large egg white

1 teaspoon ground cinnamon

¼ teaspoon kosher salt

2½ cups old-fashioned rolled oats

1 cup roughly chopped pecans (or walnuts)

½ cup wheat germ

1. Heat the oven to 325°F. Spray a large rimmed baking sheet with nonstick cooking spray.

2. In a large bowl, whisk together the maple syrup, honey, oil, egg white, cinnamon, and salt. Fold in the oats, pecans, and wheat germ until completely coated.

3. Scrape the mixture onto the baking sheet and spread it out in an even layer. Bake for 30 minutes, stirring halfway through. Use a spatula to pat the gra-noola together so it's in a tight, even layer, leaving a 1-inch border around the edges. Continue to bake until golden, 10 to 15 minutes more. Remove from the oven and immediately run a long, thin spatula underneath the gra-noola to loosen it from the baking sheet, then let it cool completely without disturbing.

4. When it's cool, use your hands to break up the gra-noola into clusters. Store in an airtight container, then scoop a scrumptious snack whenever you need one. Or add it to a bowl of yogurt and top with fruit for an easy Noolian meal!

In the Jungle of Nool
by the cool o' the poola,
even elephants drool
for this scrumptious Gra-Noola.

Pups in Cups

CHEESY MINI-POPOVERS WITH SLICED HOT DOGS

These rich, cheesy popovers hide a hot dog surprise. Make 'em warm for lunch, or save 'em for an after-school nibble.

	Nonstick cooking spray
½	cup all-purpose flour
½	teaspoon kosher salt
	Freshly ground black pepper
4	large eggs
⅓	cup whole milk
¼	cup grated Parmesan
2	tablespoons grated Gruyère
2 to 3	hot dogs, sliced into 24 pieces

1. Heat the oven to 400°F. Spray nonstick cooking spray evenly into the cups of a 24-cup mini-muffin pan.

2. In a large bowl, whisk together the flour, salt, and pepper to taste. In a medium bowl, whisk together the eggs, milk, Parmesan, and Gruyère. Pour the egg mixture into the large bowl with the dry ingredients and mix until they're just combined. Don't mix it too much!

3. Spoon about 1 tablespoon of the batter into each muffin cup, then top with a hot dog slice. Bake until your Pup Cups are puffed and set, 10 to 15 minutes. Let cool slightly. Use a small, thin spatula to pop the Pups out of the cups and serve 'em up warm!

A PUP in a CUP
(like a PIG in a BLANKET)
is LUNCH in one MUNCH
(it's DOUGH 'round
a FRANK-let).

Pup went up, and pup went down.
Then Mr. Brown flew out of town.

Downside-Up Muffins

UPSIDE-DOWN PIZZA CORN MUFFINS

It's fun to layer the ingredients in these pizza muffins—and you don't even have to stand on your head to eat them!

Extra-virgin olive oil, for greasing the pan

6 tablespoons grated Parmesan

8 tablespoons (1 stick) unsalted butter, melted

1½ cups buttermilk, or plain yogurt thinned with a little milk

2 large eggs

1 cup yellow cornmeal

½ cup whole-wheat flour

1 tablespoon baking powder

1 teaspoon kosher salt

½ teaspoon baking soda

½ cup shredded mozzarella

1¼ cups tomato sauce

⅓ cup sliced mini pepperoni or diced regular pepperoni (optional)

1. Heat the oven to 400°F. Oil a nonstick 12-cup muffin pan. Sprinkle 1½ teaspoons of Parmesan into each muffin cup. It's on the bottom now, but when you're done, it will be on top!

2. In a medium bowl, whisk together the butter, buttermilk, and eggs. In a large bowl, whisk together the cornmeal, flour, baking powder, salt, and baking soda. Stir the buttermilk mixture into the flour mixture until they're well combined.

3. Place 2 tablespoons of batter in each muffin cup. Divide the mozzarella among the muffin cups, then top with tomato sauce—a generous 1½ tablespoons in each cup. Spread the sauce in an even layer. Top with the pepperoni,

if you're using it. This will be the bottom of your pizza.

4. Bake until the muffins puff, 15 to 18 minutes. (They should spring back when you gently poke them.) Let them cool in the pan for 10 minutes. Run a thin spatula or butter knife around each muffin to loosen and gently pull it out. Now flip it over so the browned cheese is on top. Serve warm or at room temperature.

His fall was softened by his hat, so downside up, he ate his snack.

Brown and Black's Snacks

HOMEMADE HUMMUS WITH SEAWEED-SNACK CRUMBLES

Hummus is a tasty treat that's even better when shared with friends. Dip into it with pretzels, carrots, or just a spoon!

Juice of 1 small lemon

1 garlic clove, finely grated or minced

¾ teaspoon kosher salt

¼ teaspoon ground cumin

¼ cup tahini

Extra-virgin olive oil

1 14.5-ounce can of chickpeas, drained and rinsed in a colander

3 sheets of dried seaweed snacks, torn into small pieces

Whole-wheat pretzels or carrots, for serving

1. In a blender, combine the lemon juice, garlic, and salt. Let it sit for 2 minutes, then add the cumin, tahini, and 2 tablespoons of oil. Blend to combine, adding water— 1 tablespoon at a time—until it makes a very thick paste. Scrape down the sides of the blender as needed.

2. Add the chickpeas and two-thirds of the seaweed to the blender. Blend until smooth, adding 1 tablespoon of water at a time, up to 4 tablespoons, as needed to keep the mixture going (it should move around). If it gets stuck, turn off the blender and give it a poke with a rubber spatula.

3. Using a spatula, scrape or glop the hummus into a serving bowl, then drizzle it with olive oil. Top with the remaining seaweed and serve with pretzels or carrots on the side. Grab a friend and enjoy!

Brown came back with Mr. Black,
and side by side they made a snack.
Their seaweed's black, their hummus brown—
their snack has brought them great renown.

Pop's belly is round,
and so bouncy for hopping.
We've hopped till we're hungry
for toast with a topping.
Pop says that his belly
is NOT trampoline-y—
but we say it's perfect
for topping crostini!

Top on Pop

CROSTINI (ITALIAN TOAST) WITH TOPPINGS

This toast is the most, with toppings to hop for. Use the toppings listed below or come up with your own. (This toast won't complain when you drop things atop it!)

1 baguette, sliced diagonally ¼ inch thick

Extra-virgin olive oil

1 small garlic clove, cut in half crosswise (optional)

1 avocado, diced

1 teaspoon freshly squeezed lime juice

Kosher salt and freshly ground black pepper

1 large tomato, diced

3 to 4 radishes, thinly sliced

5 ounces fresh mozzarella, thinly sliced

¼ cup fresh basil leaves, torn

Flaky sea salt (optimal), for serving

1. Heat the oven to 400°F. Place the baguette slices in an even layer on a rimmed baking sheet and brush with oil. Bake until the slices are crisp and the edges are golden, about 10 minutes. Remove from the oven, let cool for a few minutes, then rub the toast lightly with the cut side of a garlic half (if you like garlic).

2. Meanwhile, in a small bowl, gently toss together the avocado, lime juice, and ¼ teaspoon salt.

3. In a separate small bowl, toss the tomato with 2 teaspoons of oil, ¼ teaspoon salt, and pepper to taste.

4. Top one-third of the toast slices with the avocado and then with radish slices.

5. Top another third of the toast slices with mozzarella slices, basil, and a drizzle of oil.

6. Spoon the tomatoes over the last third of the crostini and drizzle with more oil. Right before serving, sprinkle flaky sea salt or kosher salt over all of the crostini. That's it for the topping—now back to hopping!

PART 2

Fun That Is Yummy

For cooks who are ready to try something new,

these recipes offer a challenge or two.

With help from your grown-up, you'll soon come to see

the kitchen is truly a FUN place to be!

Warm Whisked Wocket Waffles

RYE FLOUR WAFFLES WITH MAPLE RASPBERRIES

Healthy rye flour is the perfect partner for tangy fruit and maple syrup. Make extras and freeze them for toastable breakfasts all week long.

1 cup all-purpose flour

1 cup light rye flour (or whole-wheat flour)

1 tablespoon sugar

1 teaspoon baking powder

1 teaspoon salt, plus a pinch more for the syrup

½ teaspoon baking soda

1 cup buttermilk, or plain yogurt thinned with a little milk

¾ cup whole milk

8 tablespoons (1 stick) unsalted butter, melted

4 large eggs

Nonstick cooking spray

3 tablespoons maple syrup, plus more for serving

1 cup raspberries, fresh or frozen and thawed

1. Heat the oven to 200°F. Place a rimmed baking sheet in the oven. (You'll use it to keep the waffles warm.)

2. In a large bowl, whisk together the all-purpose flour, rye flour, sugar, baking powder, salt, and baking soda. In a medium bowl, whisk together the buttermilk, milk, butter, and eggs until it's all one color. Stir the wet ingredients into the flour mixture until just combined. (Don't overmix or the waffles will be tough!)

3. Heat a waffle iron and spray it with nonstick cooking spray. Scoop ½ cup batter per waffle into the waffle iron and cook until golden, 2 to 5 minutes. Transfer the waffles to the baking sheet in the oven to keep warm while you make the rest.

4. In a small saucepan, bring the maple syrup and a pinch of salt to a low simmer over medium-low heat. Remove from the heat and stir in the raspberries.

5. To serve, transfer the waffles to serving plates and top with the maple raspberries—and more maple syrup, if you like!

Crooked Nook Hooks

ROASTED SHRIMP WITH A BUTTER, LEMON, AND GARLIC GLAZE

These simple, tasty shrimps are shaped like hooks. The glaze makes them quick to cook and quick to be gobbled!

4 tablespoons (½ stick) unsalted butter

2 garlic cloves, finely grated or minced

Finely grated zest of ½ lemon (about 1½ teaspoons)

2 pounds fresh (or frozen and thawed) large shrimp, peeled and deveined, patted dry

1½ teaspoons kosher salt

Freshly ground black pepper

Freshly squeezed lemon juice

1. Heat the oven to 475°F.

2. In a small saucepan, heat the butter and garlic over medium-low heat until the butter is melted and the garlic is fragrant, 2 to 3 minutes. Remove from the heat and stir in the lemon zest. Let cool slightly.

3. On a rimmed baking sheet, toss the shrimp with the cooled garlic butter and sprinkle with the salt and pepper to taste. Roast, tossing halfway through, until the shrimp is pink and cooked through, 4 to 6 minutes. Cool slightly, then sprinkle with lemon juice to taste. Serve warm, and your Nook will give you a happy look.

This Nook needs a hook
to hang his book
called *How to Cook.*
Since a shrimp can look
like a hook,
would you cook a hook
from this book
for the Nook?

Eggs Oobleck

SCRAMBLED EGGS WITH CREAM CHEESE AND SLICED BLACK OLIVES

The creamy, mild cheese and salty olives perk up these soft scrambled eggs. A jiggly treat for breakfast, lunch, or dinner.

10 large eggs

¼ cup milk

½ teaspoon kosher salt

Freshly ground black pepper

2 tablespoons unsalted butter

4 ounces cream cheese, softened

3 tablespoons sliced black olives

Fresh dill sprigs, for serving (optional)

1. In a large bowl, whisk the eggs with the milk, salt, and pepper to taste.

2. Melt the butter in a large nonstick skillet over medium-low heat. Pour in the egg mixture and cook, stirring frequently, until curds are evenly formed but the eggs still look wet, about 5 minutes.

Dollop in the cream cheese and fold a few times, then transfer to serving plates.

3. Top with olives and dill, if you're that kind of scrambled-egg-eater.

All the fanciest brunch foods should jiggle and quake more, like the wobblesome substance these eggs have been named for.

I will not eat them warm and cheesy.
I will not eat them over easy.
I do not like them salted twice.
I do not like them crisp and nice.
                    WAIT . . .

Green Eggs and Ham in a Skillet

CREAMY SPINACH WITH EGGS AND HAM

Adding cream and Parmesan to Green Eggs and Ham gives the dish a comforting cheesiness that'll win over any Green-Eggs-and-Ham doubter. Make a game of cracking the eggs without breaking the yolk—although broken yolks are delicious, too.

2 tablespoons unsalted butter

2 ounces cooked ham, diced

2 shallots, minced

Kosher salt and freshly ground black pepper

15 ounces fresh baby spinach

4 tablespoons heavy cream

5 tablespoons grated Parmesan

4 large eggs

1. Heat the oven to 375°F.

2. Melt the butter in a large skillet over medium heat. Add the ham (watch out for splatter!) and fry until golden and crispy around the edges, about 4 minutes. With a slotted spoon, transfer the ham to a plate.

3. Add the shallots and a pinch of salt to the skillet and cook until soft, 5 to 8 minutes. Stir in the spinach (you may have to add it in batches) and another pinch of salt; cook until the spinach wilts, about 3 minutes. Remove from the heat and stir in the cream and Parmesan.

4. With the back of a spoon, make 4 craters in the spinach mixture, and carefully crack the eggs into them. Season with salt and pepper to taste. Transfer the skillet to the oven and bake until the eggs are lightly set, 7 to 10 minutes. Sprinkle with the ham, then try them, try them, you will see!

. . . now that I say it this way, they don't sound bad—they sound okay!

Grinch Toast

FRENCH TOAST AND FRUIT ON A STICK

It's nifty to eat with no knife and fork, especially custardy kebab-style French toast. You can use any of your favorite fruits—melon, peaches, blackberries. . . . If it can be skewer-squinched, it works for Grinch Toast!

4   large eggs

1⅓   cups milk

⅓   cup heavy cream

2   tablespoons maple syrup, plus more for serving

1   teaspoon vanilla extract

¼   teaspoon freshly grated nutmeg

  Pinch of fine sea salt

1   1-pound loaf of challah or white bread, sliced 1½ inches thick

1   tablespoon unsalted butter, plus more as needed

  Cinnamon sugar (optional)

3½   cups pineapple chunks, cut into 1-inch pieces (about 24 pieces)

1   pound fresh strawberries, hulled and halved

1. Place a wire rack in a rimmed baking sheet, and set it in the oven. Heat the oven to 200°F. (You'll use the rack to keep the toast warm.)

2. In a large, shallow bowl, whisk together the eggs, milk, cream, maple syrup, vanilla, nutmeg, and salt. Dip a challah slice in the mixture and leave it for 1 minute. Then turn it over and dip the other side for 1 to 3 minutes, until the bread is squishy. Carefully transfer the squishy bread to a second rimmed baking sheet and continue with the remaining slices. Once all of them have been dipped, use a spoon to pour any remaining liquid all over the bread.

3. Melt the butter in a large nonstick skillet over medium heat. When the foam subsides, add as many soaked bread slices as will fit in one layer with space in between. Cover the skillet and cook until golden brown on the bottom, about 5 minutes. Flip and cook, covered, for another 4 minutes, or until cooked through. Transfer the French toast to the wire rack in the oven as it finishes. Repeat with the remaining bread slices, adding more butter as needed.

4. When the bread has all been cooked, cut each French toast slice into 1½-inch chunks. Sprinkle lightly with cinnamon sugar, if using. Thread the French toast pieces onto skewers, alternating them with pineapple pieces and strawberry halves, and snip the pointy ends with a pair of kitchen scissors. Serve right away. Don't be stingy with maple syrup on the side for dipping!

Now that his Grinch-heart has grown out three sizes,
the Grinch throws a brunch that is filled with surprises.
This morning his puzzler un-puzzled a trick—
that brunch is much funner when squinched on a stick.

Lorax Leaves

MIX-IT-YOURSELF SALAD BAR

Salad bars are the funnest way of salad eating—you can put exactly what you like into your bowl. Nothing yucky, only your favorite vegetables and garnishes allowed. Can you think up other ingredients that would be yummy in a salad?

FOR THE SALAD:

4	large eggs
2	cups broccoli florets
1	large carrot, coarsely shredded
½	red bell pepper, thinly sliced
¼	red onion, thinly sliced
½	cup sliced olives
8 to 10	ounces (8 cups) salad greens (like baby spinach, romaine, or spring mix)
	Shredded cheddar or Gruyère
	Crumbled blue cheese

FOR THE RANCH DRESSING:

½	cup sour cream
2	tablespoons mayonnaise
2	tablespoons minced fresh dill
1	garlic clove, finely grated or minced
⅛	teaspoon paprika
	Kosher salt and freshly ground black pepper
3	tablespoons buttermilk, or plain yogurt thinned with a little milk, or as needed

FOR THE BALSAMIC VINAIGRETTE:

1	small garlic clove, finely grated or minced
¼	cup balsamic vinegar
½	teaspoon kosher salt
¼	teaspoon freshly ground black pepper
¼	cup extra-virgin olive oil
1	teaspoon Dijon mustard
1	teaspoon honey

continues on next page

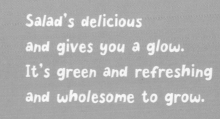

Salad's delicious
and gives you a glow.
It's green and refreshing
and wholesome to grow.

1. MAKE THE SALAD: Bring a small pot of water to a boil, then lower in the eggs. Cook for 6 minutes, adjusting the heat to maintain a simmer. Add the broccoli florets and cook for 2 minutes more. Drain in a colander and immediately run cold water over the eggs and broccoli to stop the cooking. Transfer the broccoli to a small bowl. Peel and quarter the eggs.

2. Arrange the carrot, bell pepper, onion, olives, salad greens, and cheeses in their own serving bowls to create a salad bar.

3. MAKE THE RANCH DRESSING: In a medium bowl, whisk together the sour cream, mayonnaise, dill, garlic, paprika, and salt and pepper to taste. Whisk in the buttermilk—the dressing should be runny enough to coat a salad. Taste and add more salt and pepper if needed. (It should be slightly saltier than you'd want to eat alone; the flavors will get diluted once it's on the salad.)

4. MAKE THE BALSAMIC VINAIGRETTE: In a medium bowl, whisk together the garlic, balsamic vinegar, salt, and pepper. Let it sit for a minute to mellow the flavor of the garlic, then whisk while adding the oil slowly until combined. Whisk in the mustard and honey.

5. Arrange the bowls on the table for people to make their own salads.

One fish

tuna fish

Some fish

are yum fish

One Fish, Tuna Fish!

TUNA SALAD SANDWICH

This yummy, crunchy tuna lunch will make your mouth as happy as your tummy. (And that's the best catch of all.)

1 16-inch baguette, cut crosswise into 4 equal pieces

2 tablespoons unsalted butter, melted

2 5-ounce cans of tuna, drained

¼ cup coarsely grated carrot

⅓ cup finely chopped celery

3 tablespoons mayonnaise

1 tablespoon honey mustard

½ teaspoon freshly squeezed lemon juice, plus more as needed

Kosher salt and freshly ground black pepper

4 to 6 leaves of Bibb or butter lettuce

Cornichons or other pickles, for serving

1. Place a rack 4 inches from the heat source, and heat the broiler. With a serrated knife, cut the baguette pieces ALMOST all the way through lengthwise, then spread them open with your hands so one long side is still attached (like an open book). Brush the insides with butter. Place the bread, cut side up, on a rimmed baking sheet and broil until golden, 1 to 3 minutes. Let cool.

2. In a medium bowl, fold together the tuna, carrot, celery, mayonnaise, mustard, and lemon juice. Add salt and pepper to taste and more lemon juice as needed.

3. Spread the tuna mixture across the bottom of a baguette and top with lettuce. Repeat with the other baguette pieces—one fish, two fish, three. . . . Serve with pickles on the side.

Bartholomew and the Ooey-Gooey Grilled Cheese

GRILLED CHEDDAR AND MARMALADE ON WHOLE-WHEAT BREAD

Two tangy cheeses play off the sweetness of the marmalade to make a buttery grilled-cheese sensation. However you slice it, when the cheese oozes out, the only way to stop it is to eat it up!

2½ tablespoons unsalted butter, softened

4 slices whole-wheat bread

2 tablespoons orange marmalade

2 slices American cheese

2 ounces grated extra-sharp cheddar (about ½ cup)

1. Use 2 tablespoons of the butter to slather the bread on both sides. Spread the marmalade on two of the slices, then top with American cheese. Sprinkle the grated cheddar on top. Cover with the remaining bread slices and press down firmly, without squishing.

2. Heat the remaining ½ tablespoon butter in a large nonstick skillet over medium heat. When hot, place both sandwiches in the skillet. Cover the skillet and cook until golden brown on the bottom, 3 to 4 minutes. Flip and cook on the other side, covered, for about 3 minutes more, or until the cheese is melted. Serve warm and gooey.

Imagine warm cheese raining down from the skies.
Like marmalade cheddar, a gooey surprise.
But trap it in bread? Sure, it sounds kind of screwy.
Just try it and see—it's the best kind of ooey.

Fig One and Fig Two

DRIED FIG "SALAMI"

You'll go wild for this sweet, figgy snack! Figs are easily chopped with a butter knife. And you'll have no problem shaping the log by rolling it once it's on the parchment paper.

8   ounces dried Mission figs, tough stems removed, roughly chopped (about 1¼ cups)

1   sprig of fresh rosemary

¼   cup orange juice

¼   cup water

1   tablespoon honey, plus more to taste

½   teaspoon finely grated lemon zest

½   teaspoon kosher salt, plus more to taste

¼   teaspoon fennel seeds, crushed

Pinch of ground cloves

¾   cup roughly chopped toasted walnuts (see NOTE)

Crackers, for serving

Cream cheese or cheddar, for serving

1. In a small saucepan with a tight-fitting lid, combine the figs, rosemary, orange juice, water, honey, lemon zest, salt, fennel seeds, and cloves. Bring to a simmer, cover, then continue to simmer over low heat, stirring occasionally, until the liquid is mostly evaporated, about 12 minutes. Remove from the heat and discard the rosemary sprig.

2. Scrape the fig mixture into a food processor and pulse until a thick paste forms. (If you don't have a food processor, you can chop by hand until everything is finely diced and well mixed together.) Taste and add more salt or a touch more honey, if needed.

3. Add the walnuts and pulse briefly (or chop) to combine.

4. Scrape the mixture onto a 12-inch length of parchment paper, then use the parchment to roll it into a nice, tight log. Twist the ends of the parchment to seal it, then transfer to the refrigerator. Let the log firm up overnight.

5. Unwrap the log and cut it into slices. Serve with crackers and cheese.

NOTE: To toast walnuts, heat the oven to 325°F. Spread the nuts out on a rimmed baking sheet and bake them, stirring once or twice, until they deepen in color and smell nutty, 12 to 18 minutes. Let them cool on the baking sheet before using.

These figs will not bite you.
They always taste nice.
Just roll them up tightly
and cut a big slice.

A poodle slurping noodles
from a soup bowl
spills a puddle
on the table.
That's the trouble—
because poodles
who slurp noodles
are unable
to use ladles.

Poodle Noodle Chicken Soup

CHICKEN SOUP WITH BRIGHTLY COLORED VEGGIES AND NOODLES

Chicken noodle soup is at its noodliest with tricolor pasta and sweet sugar snap peas floating in the bowl. This is a hearty soup, enough for a meal. Ladle up an oodle!

2	large chicken breasts, preferably bone-in
	Kosher salt
3	tablespoons extra-virgin olive oil
2	large carrots, halved lengthwise and sliced
2	celery stalks, sliced crosswise
½	onion, thinly sliced
3	garlic cloves, thinly sliced
4	cups low-sodium chicken broth
4	cups water
1	bay leaf
1½	teaspoons chopped fresh oregano or basil
6	ounces tricolor rotini pasta, or other bite-size pasta shape
½	cup sugar snap peas, trimmed and sliced
	Chopped fresh parsley, for serving

1. Sprinkle the chicken lightly with salt and let it sit at room temperature while you chop and slice the veggies. (This helps season it.)

2. Heat the oil in a large heavy-bottomed pot over medium-high heat. Stir in the carrots, celery, onion, garlic, and 1 teaspoon salt. Cook for about 7 minutes, or until the onion is soft.

3. Add the chicken breasts to the pot. Pour in the broth and water, then stir in the bay leaf and oregano. Bring to a simmer and cook for 15 minutes, or until the chicken is cooked through (no pink should show when you cut into the thickest part). The trick to tender chicken is maintaining a bare simmer, so adjust the heat as necessary.

4. Remove the chicken from the pot and let it cool on a cutting board. Once it's cool to the touch, shred the chicken into bite-size pieces—and discard the bones, if you've got 'em.

5. Meanwhile, bring the stock to a boil. Stir in the pasta and 1 teaspoon salt and cook for 2 minutes less than the package directions indicate. Remove from the heat and immediately stir in the snap peas. The residual heat from the stock will finish cooking the pasta and peas so they're not mushy.

6. Add the shredded chicken back to the pot. Let the soup cool slightly, then taste and add more salt if needed. Serve sprinkled with parsley, and try the tongue-twister once more.

Sleepwalking Sheep

LAMB MEATBALLS ON FLUFFY MASHED POTATO CLOUDS

Plump lamb meatballs sleep on deep heaps of mashed potatoes—
a flavor that will WAKE UP your taste buds.

FOR THE MASHED POTATO CLOUDS:

- 3 pounds white or yellow potatoes, peeled and cut into 1½-inch chunks
- Kosher salt
- ⅓ cup whole milk, plus more as needed
- 3 tablespoons unsalted butter

FOR THE MEATBALLS:

- Extra-virgin olive oil
- 1 pound ground lamb (or lean ground beef or turkey)
- 1 teaspoon kosher salt
- ¼ teaspoon freshly ground black pepper
- ¼ teaspoon ground allspice
- ¼ cup panko or other unseasoned bread crumbs
- ¼ cup grated Parmesan
- 1 large egg, lightly beaten
- Chopped fresh chives, for serving (optional)

1. MAKE THE POTATOES: Place the potatoes in a large pot. Add enough cold water to cover them by 1 inch; season the water generously with salt. Bring to a simmer and cook until the potatoes are fork-tender, 8 to 12 minutes. Drain the potatoes and return them to the pot.

2. MAKE THE MEATBALLS: While the potatoes are cooking, place an oven rack 4 inches from the heating element, and heat the broiler. Drizzle a rimmed baking sheet with oil.

3. In a large bowl, use clean hands to smoosh together the lamb, salt, pepper, allspice, panko, Parmesan, and egg until well combined. Use a cookie scoop or spoon to form 1½-inch balls (you should have 16 balls). Place on the prepared baking sheet, then drizzle with more oil. Broil until browned and cooked through, 6 to 8 minutes, shaking the baking sheet every few minutes to encourage even browning.

4. BACK TO THE POTATOES: Use a potato masher to mash in the milk, butter, and ¾ teaspoon salt. Taste and add more salt and/or milk if needed.

5. To serve, dollop the mashed potatoes onto serving plates, then nestle some meatballs in a heap on top. Sprinkle with chives, if using. A deep yummy heap!

We saw some sheep
take a walk in their sleep.
They rolled into place,
without even a bleat.
Potatoes with meatballs—
a sleepy sheep heap.

Franks and McBeans

SAUSAGE WITH TANGY TOMATO AND WHITE BEANS

This yummy variation on franks and beans will excite kids and grown-ups alike. A tiny bit of curry powder makes it extra extra.

- 2 tablespoons extra-virgin olive oil
- 4 mild turkey or pork sausages, pricked all over with a fork
- 1 small or ½ large onion, diced
- ¼ teaspoon curry powder, plus more to taste

  Kosher salt

  Freshly ground black pepper
- 2 garlic cloves, finely grated or minced
- 1 tablespoon tomato paste
- 1 14.5-ounce can of cannellini beans, drained and rinsed in a colander
- 1 14.5-ounce can of diced tomatoes

1. Heat the oil in a large skillet over medium-high heat. Add the sausages and cook, turning occasionally, until well browned, about 12 minutes. Transfer to a plate and reduce the heat to medium.

2. Stir in the onion, curry powder, ½ teaspoon salt, and pepper to taste, and cook until the onion starts to brown around the edges, about 8 minutes. Stir in the garlic and tomato paste and cook until fragrant, 1 to 2 minutes. Stir in the beans, tomatoes, and ¼ teaspoon salt. Fill the tomato can one-third full with water and stir it into the skillet.

3. Add the sausages to the skillet in a single layer, bring to a simmer, and cook until the sauce has thickened, 15 to 20 minutes. Taste and add more salt and curry powder if you like.

4. To serve, transfer the sausages to serving plates and top with the bean-and-tomato mixture.

The Sneetches cooked frankfurters, roasting in rhythm.
Just one thing was missing: "Now, what to serve with 'em?"
They eyed old McBean as he packed his machines.
Inspired, they roasted McFranks with McBeans.

Gooey goo for chewy chewing!
That's what that Goo-Goose is doing.
If you choose to chew goo, too,
then only true Blue Goo will do!

Chewy Blue Goo

HOMEMADE BLUEBERRY GELATIN

Brew blueberries into this fruity goo-berry gelatin, and you will choose to chew goo, too.

1½ cups blueberry juice, blueberry juice cocktail, or purple grape juice

1 tablespoon unflavored powdered gelatin

2 to 3 tablespoons sugar or honey

Nonstick cooking spray

Whipped cream, for serving (optional)

1. Place a silicone mini Bundt mold with 6 cavities on a small rimmed baking sheet.

2. In a medium bowl, whisk together ¼ cup of the juice and the gelatin. Let it sit until the gelatin "blooms" (thickens and turns into see-through goo).

3. Pour another ¼ cup of the juice and the sugar into a microwave-safe bowl or measuring cup and heat in the microwave until steaming. Carefully stir the hot juice until the sugar dissolves. Pour it over the bloomed gelatin goo and mix to combine. Stir in the remaining 1 cup of fruit juice.

4. Pour the mixture into the cavities of the mini Bundt mold and refrigerate for at least 4 hours, until it's firm and jiggly. Overnight is even better.

5. Now to unmold the gelatin—Blue Goo is sticky! Spray a small rimmed baking sheet or a tray with nonstick cooking spray. Fill a casserole dish or baking pan with warm water, high enough so it comes ALMOST to the top of the silicone mold. Lower the mold into the water, open side up, and leave it for about 45 seconds, then turn it over onto the prepared baking sheet. The gelatin should slide right out; if it doesn't, return it to the water for another 15 seconds.

6. Keep the gelatin on the baking sheet in the fridge until ready to serve, or transfer it right away to serving plates (the Goo starts to slouch if left out too long). Top with whipped cream for a showstopping topping!

Eleven Fingers. Eleven!

CLASSIC CHICKEN FINGERS THAT ARE BAKED, NOT FRIED

Baking these chicken fingers is easier and healthier than frying, and the Parmesan crust makes them especially rich. However many you make, this dish is always a perfect 10! (Plus one.)

1¼	cups panko or other unseasoned bread crumbs
½	cup grated Parmesan
	Kosher salt
	Freshly ground black pepper
	Extra-virgin olive oil
½	cup all-purpose flour
¼	teaspoon paprika
2	large eggs
1¼	pounds chicken tenders, or chicken breast sliced lengthwise in thin strips
	Ketchup or lemon wedges, for serving (optional)

1. Place a rimmed baking sheet in the oven, and heat the oven to 425°F.

2. In a large, shallow bowl, stir together the panko, Parmesan, a large pinch of salt, and pepper to taste. Stir in 1 tablespoon oil and toss until the crumbs are evenly coated.

3. In another shallow bowl, stir together the flour, paprika, and a pinch of salt. Crack the eggs into a third shallow bowl, add a pinch of salt, and beat well with a fork or whisk.

4. Now for the Finger Batter Factory Line! Arrange your assembly line in this order: flour, eggs, bread crumbs, and then a second baking sheet with a wire rack on it. Sprinkle the chicken with salt and pepper. Dip the chicken pieces first in the flour, then in the eggs (shaking off the excess), and then in the bread crumbs, coating the chicken completely at every step. When each piece is breaded, place it on the prepared wire rack to wait for its fellow fingers to be finished.

5. When all the fingers are ready, carefully remove the hot baking sheet from the oven and drizzle it with oil. Place the breaded chicken pieces on the baking sheet and return it to the oven. Bake until golden and cooked through, about 11 minutes, flipping after 6 minutes. Let cool, then serve with ketchup or lemon wedges on the side, if you like.

We LOVE chicken fingers—
we're such finger fans
that counting the reasons
would take both our hands.

Patented Fruit *Pfoosh*

APPLE-PEAR SAUCE WITH MAPLE SYRUP AND CINNAMON

Applesauce is all well and good, but apple-pear *pfoosh* is *pfantastic*! A splash of maple syrup and cinnamon give it sweetness and zing.

2 pounds sweet apples (such as Golden Delicious or Fuji), peeled, cored, and diced

1 pound pears, peeled, cored, and diced

2 to 4 tablespoons maple syrup

1 3-inch cinnamon stick

Pinch of kosher salt

½ cup water

1 to 2 teaspoons freshly squeezed lemon juice

1. In a large pot, combine the apples, pears, 2 tablespoons maple syrup, cinnamon stick, salt, and water. Bring to a simmer, then cover and simmer over low heat until the apples are tender, about 30 minutes. Stir occasionally to make sure the fruit doesn't burn.

2. Uncover and continue to simmer until most of the liquid is gone, about 12 minutes. Discard the cinnamon stick.

3. Transfer to a food processor. Add lemon juice to taste, and process until smooth. Taste and add more lemon juice and maple syrup if you like. Serve, or store in an airtight container in the fridge for up to 5 days. Have *pfun* when you eat it, but don't leave it around!

Pat sat down dreaming of apples and pears,
the day he left apples and pears on his chair.
When Pat stood back up, that's when *pfooshing* was Patented.
We call a fruit *pfooshed* after someone has sat in it.

Yertle the Torta

SWEET PHYLLO TORTA WITH COTTAGE CHEESE AND HONEY

Think of this as a cheesecake with crunch. The phyllo pastry on the outside is like a turtle's shell—except yummy—encasing the sweet, creamy cheese inside.

20 ounces (2½ cups) cottage cheese (4 percent fat)

4 ounces cream cheese, softened

3 large eggs

3 tablespoons sugar

¼ teaspoon kosher salt

8 tablespoons (1 stick) unsalted butter, melted

1 1-pound box of frozen phyllo dough, thawed in the refrigerator

Full-flavored honey, such as wildflower, for drizzling

1. Heat the oven to 400°F. In a food processor or a stand mixer, blend together half of the cottage cheese, and the cream cheese, eggs, sugar, and salt. Scrape into a large bowl and fold in the remaining cottage cheese.

2. Brush a 10-inch Bundt pan with some of the melted butter. Stack 2 sheets of phyllo, poke a hole in the center, and fit the sheets into the Bundt pan, fitting the hole over the middle tube. Press the sheets against the sides of the pan and let the corners hang over the edge. Repeat with 2 more sheets, rotating the corners so they hang perpendicular to the first sheets. Continue with the remaining phyllo.

3. Spoon the filling into the phyllo dough, then fold the phyllo edges over the filling. Pour the remaining melted butter evenly over the phyllo and around the edges. Place the Bundt pan on a rimmed baking sheet and bake until golden, about 1 hour. Let the torta cool in the pan for about 1 hour, then invert it onto a plate and drizzle it royally with honey. Slice, drizzle with more honey if you like, and serve warm.

This torta is sorta like Yertle, I reckon,
king for one day, and then gone by the second.
A cheesecake that's crunchy, you just can't go wrong!
This torta-shell treat surely won't last too long.

STEW

Mr. Brown learned to MOO,
and then his talents GREW.
Now Mr. Brown can STEW.
If Brown can—so can YOU!

Mr. Brown Can Stew! Can YOU?

LEMONY BEEF STEW OVER A MOUND OF WHOLE-WHEAT COUSCOUS

Stewing takes time, but it's well worth learning how. You can make this rich beef stew and refrigerate it for nourishing meals all week long.

3   tablespoons extra-virgin olive oil

3   pounds beef stew meat, cut into 2-inch cubes

Kosher salt and freshly ground black pepper

1   onion, diced

1   large carrot, peeled and diced

4   garlic cloves, finely grated or minced

1   teaspoon minced fresh thyme

1   bay leaf

Finely grated zest of 1 lemon

1   teaspoon red wine vinegar

4   cups beef stock

1   cup whole-wheat or regular couscous

1   lemon, cut in half, for serving

Chopped fresh parsley or cilantro, for serving

1. Heat the oven to 325°F. In a large Dutch oven or other heavy-bottomed ovenproof pot, heat the oil over medium-high heat. Sprinkle the beef all over with 1 tablespoon salt and ½ teaspoon pepper. Carefully put the beef in the pot in a single layer. (You may have to work in batches.) Cook until well browned, 2 to 3 minutes per side. Transfer the beef to a plate as it finishes.

2. Reduce the heat to medium and stir in the onion, carrot, garlic, and a large pinch of salt. Cook until the onion is translucent, about 8 minutes. Stir in the thyme, bay leaf, lemon zest, vinegar, stock, and browned beef. Scrape any browned bits from the bottom of the pot and bring the liquid to a simmer. Partially cover the pot, transfer it to the oven, and bake until the beef is tender, stirring occasionally, 2½ to 3 hours (yes, *hours*!). (If it starts to look dry, add ½ cup water, stir, and fully cover the pot.) Remove the bay leaf and discard.

3. While the beef is cooking, in a medium pot bring 1½ cups water and a generous pinch of salt to a boil. Remove from the heat, stir in the couscous, and cover. Let steam for 5 minutes. Fluff with a fork, then re-cover and keep warm.

4. To serve, top the couscous with the beef stew. Finish with a squeeze of lemon juice and a sprinkle of chopped parsley or cilantro. Now, YOU, too, can stew!

Truffula Fruits
with Truffully Trimmings

FROZEN CHOCOLATE-COVERED BANANAS

Truffula Fruits are a frozen delight, and all you need to grow them is chocolate, trimmings, and imagination. Truffula Fruits work just as well with strawberries instead of bananas.

1   12-ounce bag of semisweet chocolate chips

1   tablespoon coconut or neutral oil, such as sunflower or grapeseed

3   large ripe bananas, peeled and cut into 1-inch-thick slices

POSSIBLE TRUFFULLY TRIMMINGS:

Toasted shredded coconut

Sprinkles

Chopped toasted nuts

Crushed pretzels or saltines

1. Line a rimmed baking sheet with parchment paper.

2. In a medium microwave-safe bowl, microwave the chocolate on medium-low power in 30-second intervals, stirring in between, until melted. Stir in the oil with a spatula.

3. Set up your Bar-ba-loot Fruit-Trimming Line: Place the banana slices on one side, followed by the bowl of chocolate, then bowls of trimmings. Place the lined baking sheet at the end.

4. Spear a banana slice with a fork; dip it into the chocolate, then tap off the excess chocolate. Drop the slice into one of the bowls of trimmings, sprinkling on more trimming to coat. Use a clean fork to transfer the slice to the baking sheet. Repeat with the remaining banana slices and desired trimmings. (If the chocolate gets too hard, you can reheat it in the microwave for 15 seconds.)

5. Place the baking sheet in the freezer until frozen, at least 1 hour. Quickly peel the pieces off the parchment and store in a large resealable bag in the freezer. The frozen Truffula Fruits will keep for up to 3 months.

While frisking all day
in their Bar-ba-loot suits,
the Brown Bar-ba-loots
snack on Truffula Fruits.
If you have been frisking
and feel Bar-ba-loot-ish,
you must have a taste of this
chocolatey fruit dish.

You see, sour alone
is hardly a treat,
but sour's perfection
when paired up with sweet.

Sour Kangaroo

SWEET-AND-SOUR PORK TENDERLOIN

Sweet and sour are best friends in this tangy dinner!

3   garlic cloves, finely grated or minced

Kosher salt

¼   teaspoon freshly ground black pepper

¼   cup toasted sesame oil, plus more as needed

1   1¼-pound pork tenderloin, fat trimmed

1   onion, cut into 1-inch chunks

1   red bell pepper, cut into 1-inch pieces

1½   cups fresh pineapple chunks

¼   cup ketchup

¼   cup rice wine vinegar

3 to 4   tablespoons light brown sugar

2   scallions, thinly sliced, white and green parts separated

1   teaspoon low-sodium soy sauce

½   teaspoon cornstarch

1. In a large bowl, combine two-thirds of the garlic, 1 teaspoon salt, the pepper, and 1 tablespoon sesame oil. Add pork and turn to coat. Cover the bowl and chill at least 2 hours. Remove from the fridge while preparing the vegetables.

2. Arrange racks in the upper and lower thirds of the oven, and heat to 375°F. On a rimmed baking sheet, toss onion, bell pepper, and 1 cup pineapple with 2 tablespoons oil and ¼ teaspoon salt.

3. Heat remaining tablespoon oil in a large ovenproof skillet over medium-high heat. Place tenderloin in the skillet, and slide it into the oven on the top rack. Put vegetables onto the bottom rack. Cook for 15 minutes.

4. Take skillet out of the oven and carefully flip tenderloin. Stir vegetables. Return skillet to the oven. Cook until pork

reaches 140°F on an instant-read thermometer, about 10 more minutes.

5. Meanwhile, make the sauce: In a blender, combine remaining ½ cup pineapple, ketchup, vinegar, 3 tablespoons brown sugar, scallion whites, soy sauce, cornstarch, and 2 tablespoons water. Taste and add more sugar if needed. The sauce should taste tangy and sweet.

6. When the tenderloin is done, transfer it to a plate and tent with foil. Scrape sauce into the same skillet and cook over medium-high heat until it bubbles, about 2 minutes. (Watch out for the hot pan handle!) Stir in vegetables and any juices from the plate, and remove skillet from the heat.

7. Slice the tenderloin ½ inch thick and serve with the saucy vegetables and scallion greens.

Star-Belly Peaches

BAKED PEACHES STUFFED WITH CARDAMOM-WALNUT MARZIPAN, SOME WITH MINT STARS

The Sneetches agree that these baked peaches make a fun fruity dessert. Compare the plain-belly peaches to the ones with mint stars upon thars and you'll see—what matters most is what's inside.

1 **cup toasted walnuts, almonds, or pistachios (see NOTE on page 76)**

2 **tablespoons maple syrup**

½ **teaspoon ground cardamom**

Large pinch of kosher salt

4 **ripe peaches, halved and pitted**

Turbinado (raw) sugar or granulated sugar

3 **sprigs of fresh mint**

Powdered sugar (optional)

1. Heat the oven to 400°F. Line a rimmed baking sheet with parchment paper.

2. Make the marzipan: In a small food processor or blender, blend the nuts, maple syrup, cardamom, and salt to a paste. Scrape down the sides if necessary. (This might take a while, so be patient!)

3. Place the peaches, cut side up, on the prepared baking sheet. Drizzle generously with maple syrup. Stuff 1 tablespoon of the marzipan into each peach. Sprinkle with sugar.

4. Bake until the peaches are soft, 12 to 17 minutes. Let cool slightly, then sprinkle lightly with powdered sugar, if using. Place several mint leaves arranged in a star shape upon half of thars. Don't worry— they'll still get along. Peaches are peaches! Serve warm.

Some of these peaches have bellies with stars upon.
But unlike the Sneetches, our peaches have marzipan.
I'm not really sure that the stars make a difference.
It's what lies inside 'em that makes 'em splendiferous!

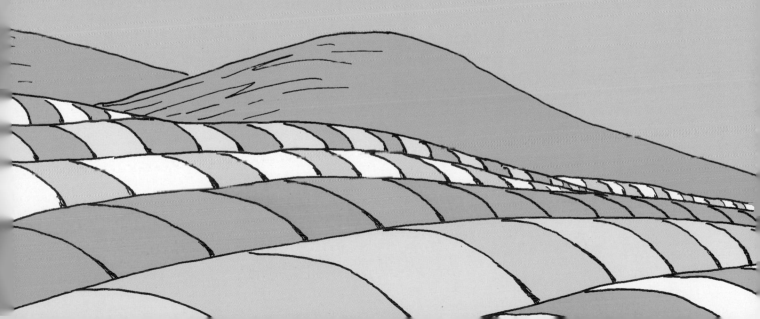

PART 3

Oh, the Dishes You'll Cook

And now we move up
to the snazziest dishes.
You'll need lots of skills.
Oh, this food is ambitious!

Eggs that jiggle here to there,
eggs that wobble everywhere.
Would you eat them on a muffin?
Would you like to pile the stuff in?

Green Eggs and Ham Here, There, and Everywhere

SCRAMBLED SPINACH EGGS AND HAM ON ENGLISH MUFFINS

Cheesy green eggs are a nutritious way to start your day. Don't worry if they wobble!

8   large eggs

2   ounces baby spinach leaves (2 packed cups), chopped

    Pinch of kosher salt

1   tablespoon unsalted butter, plus more as needed

4   slices thick-cut cooked ham

½   cup grated Parmesan (optional)

4   whole-wheat English muffins, split and toasted

1. In a blender, combine the eggs, spinach, and salt, and blend until smooth.

2. In a large nonstick skillet, melt ½ tablespoon of the butter over medium heat. Fry the ham slices until they turn golden and crisp at the edges, 3 to 5 minutes. Transfer them with a spatula to a plate.

3. Add the remaining ½ tablespoon butter to the skillet, let it melt, then stir in the egg mixture. Cook until the eggs start to set. (They go from runny to gloopy.) Sprinkle in the Parmesan, if using, and continue to cook until the eggs are set (going from gloopy to wobbly) but still soft, stirring frequently to create large curds. Remove from the heat.

4. Now build the sandwiches! Butter the English muffins if you like, then cover each bottom piece with a slice of ham and top with a mound of eggs. (It's okay if the eggs cascade off the English muffins.) Add the muffin tops and serve. You can eat this with a fork to keep the eggs from wobbling everywhere.

105

Katroo Birthday Breakfast Banquet

CORNMEAL MAPLE BLUEBERRY MINI PANCAKES TOPPED WITH BACON

What's more fun for breakfast than pancakes? Pancakes made Katroo-style, that's what! Sprinkle the blueberries onto the batter and arrange the bacon into stripes.

- 8 ounces thick-cut bacon strips
- ½ cup cornmeal
- ½ cup whole-wheat flour
- 1 teaspoon baking powder
- ½ teaspoon baking soda
- ¼ teaspoon kosher salt
- 1¼ cups buttermilk, or plain yogurt thinned with a little milk
- 1 large egg
- 1 tablespoon maple syrup, plus more for serving
- 1 tablespoon unsalted butter, plus more as needed
- 1 cup blueberries, or to taste

1. Heat the oven to 375°F. Lay the bacon on a rimmed baking sheet in a single layer, then bake until browned and crispy, 16 to 22 minutes. Transfer to a paper towel–lined plate. Reduce the oven temperature to 200°F (for keeping the pancakes warm).

2. Meanwhile, in a large bowl, whisk together the cornmeal, flour, baking powder, baking soda, and salt.

3. In a medium bowl, whisk together the buttermilk, egg, and maple syrup. Scrape into the flour mixture and whisk until just combined. Let it sit for at least 5 minutes while you go on to the next step.

4. Heat a large cast-iron skillet or griddle over medium heat until very hot. Melt the butter in the skillet, then pour in ¼ cup of batter (you should be able to fit 2 or 3 in the skillet). Scatter some blueberries onto the pancakes and cook until the edges look dry, 2 to 3 minutes. Flip and cook for another 2 to 3 minutes, until golden brown and cooked through. Transfer the pancakes to a baking sheet and keep them warm in the oven. Repeat until you've used all the batter, letting the skillet get very hot again between each batch.

5. Transfer the pancakes to plates. Drizzle with maple syrup, then top each serving with 2 or 3 strips of bacon, laying them across in stripes. Serve with more maple syrup on the side.

I bet we could do what they do in Katroo,
where they know how to say "Happy birthday to you!"
We'll start your day right, with a big pile of pancakes—
watch the Birthday Bird land in the short time this plan takes.

Wickersham Biscuits

WHOLE-WHEAT BISCUITS WITH STRAWBERRY BUTTER

The strawberry butter on these buttery biscuits is too good not to share. Just make sure to mix enough for everyone!

FOR THE BISCUITS:

- 2¼ cups whole-wheat flour, plus more for dusting
- 2 teaspoons baking powder
- 1 teaspoon baking soda
- ½ teaspoon kosher salt
- 7 tablespoons cold unsalted butter, cubed
- ¾ cup buttermilk, or plain yogurt thinned with a little milk
- 1 tablespoon unsalted butter, melted

FOR THE STRAWBERRY BUTTER:

- 8 tablespoons (1 stick) unsalted butter, softened
- 1 cup (about 5 ounces) room-temperature strawberries, hulled and diced
- ½ to 1½ tablespoons maple syrup, depending on the sweetness of the strawberries
- Pinch of kosher salt

1. Heat the oven to 400°F. Line a rimmed baking sheet with parchment paper.

2. MAKE THE BISCUITS: In the bowl of a stand mixer fitted with the paddle attachment, combine the flour, baking powder, baking soda, and salt. Add the cold cubed butter and mix on medium-low speed until the mixture is sandy with a few medium-size crumbs. (Or do this in a bowl, using two knives or a pastry cutter to cut the butter into the dry ingredients and then mixing the buttermilk in with a wooden spoon.)

3. Drizzle in the buttermilk and continue to mix on medium-low until a shaggy dough forms. Transfer to a lightly floured work surface. Pat the dough together, then roll it out to a ½-inch-thick rectangle. Fold the dough over itself in half, then turn it 90 degrees and roll it out again to a ½-inch thickness, about a 5-by-10-inch rectangle.

4. Cut into eight 2½-inch squares. Transfer to the prepared baking sheet and brush the tops with melted butter. Bake until golden brown on the bottom and edges, 13 to 15 minutes.

5. MAKE THE STRAWBERRY BUTTER: For a smooth texture, use a food processor to mix together the butter, strawberries, maple syrup, and salt until combined and fluffy. Or, starting with a clean bowl, use a handheld mixer and combine for a strawberry butter that's a bit chunkier.

6. To serve, split the biscuits and smear them with strawberry butter. Any leftover strawberry butter will keep in the fridge for up to 2 weeks, or in the freezer for up to 3 months.

When Wickersham brothers and Wickersham sisters can all work together, they're fine biscuit mixers. They work side by side when they're blending the batter— but sharing the butter's a whole other matter.

Guac in Socks

HOMEMADE TORTILLA CHIPS AND GUACAMOLE

The only way to defend yourself against this irresistible guacamole is to arm yourself with even tastier homemade chips. Once you do, you will never again suffer from the shock of guac in your sock, frock, or smock.

Neutral oil, such as sunflower or grapeseed

12 corn tortillas, cut into quarters

Kosher salt and freshly ground black pepper

½ red onion, finely diced

2 garlic cloves, finely grated or minced

Juice of 1 lime

¼ teaspoon ground cumin

2 avocados, diced

1 small tomato, diced (about ½ cup)

¼ cup chopped fresh cilantro (optional)

1. Heat ½ inch of oil in a large skillet over medium-high heat to 350°F. Using a slotted spoon or tongs, slip in the tortilla pieces, 3 or 4 at a time, and fry until light golden, flipping halfway through, 1 to 2 minutes per side. Transfer the chips to a paper towel–lined plate and immediately sprinkle them with salt to taste. Repeat with the remaining tortillas, layering them between paper towels.

2. In a large bowl, combine the onion, garlic, lime juice, and cumin. Let it sit for 1 minute to mellow the flavors, then mash in the avocados, ½ teaspoon salt, and a large pinch of pepper. Fold in the tomato and cilantro, if using. Taste and add more salt if needed.

3. Transfer the chips to a serving bowl and serve with the guac right away. Leftover tortilla chips can be stored in an airtight container.

There is guac in my sock,
so I squawk when I walk.
But my doc has a tip:
scoop the guac with a chip!
Keep a grip as you dip
and your chip will not slip.

Bar-ba-loot Roots

ROASTED VEGGIES WITH PARMESAN CRUST

These roasted veggies are sweet and soft on the inside and salty and cheesy on the outside, with yummy crisp edges that turn golden brown. Bar-ba-loot roots fuel fabulous frolics!

3 parsnips, halved lengthwise and cut into 1-inch chunks

3 carrots, peeled, halved lengthwise, and cut into 1-inch chunks

1 sweet potato, peeled and cut into 1-inch chunks

2 tablespoons extra-virgin olive oil

½ teaspoon kosher salt

¼ teaspoon freshly ground black pepper

⅓ cup grated Parmesan

Chopped fresh parsley, for serving

1. Heat the oven to 400°F. On a rimmed baking sheet, toss together the parsnips, carrots, sweet potato, oil, salt, and pepper. Bake for 20 minutes, then toss the vegetables and sprinkle with the Parmesan.

2. Continue to bake until the vegetables are browned and the cheese is golden, another 15 to 20 minutes.

3. Let cool slightly on the baking sheet, then use a spatula to scrape up the vegetables and crispy cheesy bits stuck to the pan. Sprinkle with parsley and serve immediately.

The Bar-ba-*loots* frolic on neat little feets
and use them to dig in the ground for their treats.
They poke with their toes for the roots that they eat:
Crisp cheese on the outside, while inside they're sweet.

Ish's Wish Knish

SWEET POTATO–FILLED MINI PASTRIES

Crispy on the outside and soft on the inside, these sweet potato–filled pastries will make your lips smack. Make them vanish with a big munch, munch!

FOR THE DOUGH:

- 2 cups all-purpose flour
- ¾ teaspoon baking powder
- ½ teaspoon kosher salt
- ½ cup warm water
- 1 large egg yolk
- ⅓ cup neutral oil, such as sunflower or grapeseed

FOR THE FILLING:

- 2 medium sweet potatoes, peeled and cut into 2-inch chunks
- Kosher salt and freshly ground black pepper
- 2 tablespoons extra-virgin olive oil
- 2 tablespoons unsalted butter
- 1 medium onion, finely diced
- 2 garlic cloves, finely grated or minced
- 1 large egg

1. MAKE THE DOUGH: In a large bowl, whisk together the flour, baking powder, and salt. In a medium bowl, whisk together the water, egg yolk, and oil. Stir the wet mixture into the dry ingredients until a shaggy dough forms. Turn the dough out onto a lightly floured surface and knead until smooth. Return the dough to the bowl, cover with plastic wrap, and let it sit at room temperature for 1 hour.

2. MEANWHILE, MAKE THE FILLING: Place the sweet potatoes and 1 teaspoon salt in a medium pot and cover with cold water by at least 1 inch. Bring to a simmer and cook until the potatoes are tender, 8 to 12 minutes. Drain and return to the pot.

3. In a large skillet, heat the oil and butter over medium-high heat. Stir in the onion and cook, stirring frequently, until starting to brown, 10 to 12 minutes. Stir in the garlic and cook until fragrant, another 2 minutes. Scrape into the pot with the drained potatoes, add ½ teaspoon salt and a large pinch of pepper, and mash together. Let the mixture cool to room temperature. Add more salt, if needed, and pepper to taste.

4. Heat the oven to 375°F. Line a baking sheet with parchment paper. In a small bowl, make an egg wash by whisking the egg with 1 tablespoon water.

5. Cut the dough in half. Cover one half with a clean kitchen towel. On a lightly floured

continues on next page

surface, roll out the other half until it is ⅛-inch thick. Use a 3-inch cookie cutter or drinking glass to cut out rounds of dough.

6. Place some water in a small bowl and keep it nearby. Using a cookie scoop or a spoon, scoop about 2 tablespoons of potatoes into the center of each dough round. Dip your fingers in the water and wet the edge of the dough, then pull the dough up around the potatoes. Make mini folds in the dough, crimping them together to make them stick. (The potatoes will peek out of the top, and that's fine; they will look like Chinese dumplings.) Place on the prepared baking sheet. Repeat with the remaining dough and potatoes, rerolling any dough scraps.

7. When they're all done, brush the dough with egg wash and bake until golden, 20 to 25 minutes. Cool slightly before serving. Swish, swish!

Ish has a dish
to help him wish.
He waves his hand
with a big swish-swish.
Ta-da—a knish!
A knish on his dish.

Once you have
raked the fish,
and baked the fish,
and heaped the fish
upon a dish,
it's time to eat.
Now THAT'S delish!

Fish on a Rake

TERIYAKI-GLAZED FISH KEBABS WITH TUNA, BELL PEPPERS, PINEAPPLE, AND TOMATOES

The sweetness of the teriyaki sauce brings the fish together with the fruit and vegetables to make this a scrumptious one-dish meal.

FOR THE TERIYAKI SAUCE:

- 2 tablespoons mirin (sweet Japanese rice wine for cooking)
- ⅓ cup low-sodium soy sauce
- 2 teaspoons rice vinegar
- ½ tablespoon honey
- 1 garlic clove, finely grated or minced
- 1 teaspoon grated fresh ginger

FOR THE KEBABS:

- 1 pound fresh tuna, cut into 1¼-inch cubes
- 1 green bell pepper, cut into 1-inch-ish triangles
- 1 cup pineapple chunks
- 1 cup cherry tomatoes

1. MAKE THE TERIYAKI SAUCE: Put all the sauce ingredients in a small saucepan. Bring to a simmer over medium heat and reduce until thick and syrupy, 7 to 10 minutes. Let cool.

2. Put the tuna in a bowl and toss with just enough of the cooled teriyaki sauce to coat the fish. (You might not need all of it.) Cover the bowl and marinate in the refrigerator for at least 30 minutes and up to 3 hours.

3. MAKE THE KEBABS: Heat the broiler. Line a rimmed baking sheet with foil. Make kebabs by skewering each ingredient on its own skewer. Broil on the baking sheet until browned, turning every 2 minutes or so; about 4 minutes for the tuna and 10 minutes for the vegetables and pineapple chunks. Remove from skewers to serve.

NOTE: You can substitute salmon, or even chicken breast, for the tuna. If using chicken, add a few minutes to the cooking time to cook it all the way through.

Up-Up-Up with a Chicken Taco

CHICKEN TACOS WITH SALSA

Crispy broiled chicken is folded into soft, warm tortillas with salsa, cheddar, and lettuce in this fast-to-make, fun-to-eat taco. (Psst: if a Fish isn't watching, you can use salmon instead of chicken.)

2 tablespoons freshly squeezed lime juice (from 1 to 2 limes)

2 tablespoons extra-virgin olive oil

1¼ teaspoons kosher salt

½ teaspoon paprika

¼ teaspoon ground cumin

⅛ teaspoon ground cinnamon

1½ pounds boneless, skinless chicken breasts

8 flour or corn tortillas

FOR SERVING:

Prepared salsa

Shredded cheddar

Shredded lettuce

Sour cream

Lime wedges

1. In a large bowl, whisk together the lime juice, oil, salt, paprika, cumin, and cinnamon.

2. Lay a sheet of plastic wrap on a cutting board and place the chicken breasts on top, leaving a little space between them. Cover with another sheet of plastic wrap, then pound the chicken with a meat mallet or rolling pin to an even ½-inch thickness. Unwrap and place in the lime marinade, turning to coat. Cover and marinate at room temperature for 30 minutes while you prepare all the taco accompaniments.

3. Place a rack 6 inches from the heat source, and heat the broiler (or heat a grill to high). Line a rimmed baking sheet with foil, if broiling. Broil or grill the chicken until cooked, flipping halfway through, 4 to 5 minutes per side. Transfer to a cutting board to rest for 5 minutes.

4. While the chicken is resting, lay 4 tortillas out in an even layer on a rimmed baking sheet. Broil until warmed and lightly charred in spots, 1 to 2 minutes. Flip and broil for another 1 to 2 minutes. (If you're grilling, place the tortillas directly on the grill.) Transfer to a serving plate and cover with a clean kitchen towel to keep warm. Repeat with the remaining tortillas.

5. Slice the chicken into strips and transfer to a serving platter. Serve with warm tortillas, salsa, cheese, lettuce, sour cream, and lime wedges.

"Put me down!" said the Fish.
"I'm no snack for a cat!
Put me down!" said the Fish.
"Do not eye me like that!"
"Have no fear!" said the Cat.
"You will like this Cat's motto:
It's chicken (not fish)
that goes best in a taco."

Who-ville Sliders

SLIDERS WITH SLOPPY JOE FILLING

These sliders may be mini, but they have a giant taste. They are super saucy, super savory, and super sloppy. If you're not Who-sized, you'll want to eat more than one.

1 tablespoon extra-virgin olive oil

1 pound lean ground beef or turkey

Kosher salt

1 small onion, diced

2 celery stalks, diced

½ red bell pepper, diced

2 garlic cloves, finely grated or minced

1 tablespoon tomato paste

1 14.5-ounce can of crushed tomatoes

1 tablespoon dark brown sugar

1 tablespoon Worcestershire sauce

1 teaspoon apple cider vinegar

1 teaspoon powdered mustard

12 slider buns or mini dinner rolls

3 tablespoons unsalted butter, melted

1. Heat the oil in a large skillet over medium-high heat. Stir in the ground meat and ½ teaspoon salt and cook, breaking up the meat with a spoon, until browned, 10 to 15 minutes. Use a slotted spoon to scoop the meat into a bowl, leaving the fat in the skillet.

2. Add the onion, celery, and bell pepper to the skillet, cook, stirring, until the onion starts to brown, about 6 minutes. Stir in the garlic and tomato paste and cook for 2 minutes more, or until fragrant. Stir in the crushed tomatoes, sugar, Worcestershire sauce, vinegar, powdered mustard, ½ teaspoon salt, and the browned meat. Bring to a simmer and cook until the sauce has thickened, about 20 minutes. Taste and add more salt if needed.

3. Meanwhile, place a rack 4 inches from the heat source, and heat the broiler. Cut the buns in half with a serrated knife and brush the insides with butter. Toast under the broiler, cut side up, until golden, 1 to 2 minutes. Watch them carefully so they don't burn. Let them cool.

4. Serve the sloppy joe mixture on the toasted buns, giving each person 2 or 3 sliders.

Who-foods can cause you to feel much, much taller.
Who-sliders taste jumbo but look a bit smaller.

Big Bowl of Bow Ties

BOW-TIE PASTA WITH TOMATO SAUCE AND RICOTTA

Help Little Cats A to Z get dressed by making a whole bowl of Cat Bow Ties. Bow-tie pasta with red (sauce) and white (cheese) is the Cat in the Hat's Little Cats' meow!

Kosher salt

12 ounces bow-tie (farfalle) pasta

3 tablespoons extra-virgin olive oil

½ small onion, diced

2 garlic cloves, finely grated or minced

2 tablespoons tomato paste

1 28-ounce can of crushed tomatoes

1 large sprig of fresh basil, leaves torn

½ cup panko or other unseasoned bread crumbs

¼ cup grated Parmesan

¼ cup chopped fresh basil (optional)

8 ounces fresh ricotta

1. Bring a large pot of heavily salted water to a boil. Cook the pasta according to the package directions. Keep 1 cup of the pasta water for later, then drain the pasta.

2. While the pasta cooks, heat 2 tablespoons of the oil in a large skillet over medium-high heat. Stir in the onion and cook until soft and starting to brown, about 6 minutes. Stir in the garlic and tomato paste and cook until the tomato paste caramelizes and turns brick red, 1 to 2 minutes. Stir in the crushed tomatoes and torn basil and bring to a simmer. Reduce the heat and simmer until thickened and saucy, 20 to 30 minutes.

3. Stir the cooked pasta into the sauce, tossing well to coat. If the sauce looks too thick, stir in some of the reserved pasta water, a few tablespoons at a time.

4. In a medium bowl, toss together the remaining 1 tablespoon oil, the panko, and a large pinch of salt. Heat a small skillet over medium heat, then stir in the panko and cook, stirring frequently, until golden brown, 3 to 5 minutes. Scrape into a bowl and stir in the Parmesan and the chopped basil, if using.

5. To serve, mound the pasta on serving plates. Top with generous dollops of ricotta and sprinkle with the toasted panko.

Bow ties on Cats
are a marvelous sight.
And the Cats in my hat
wear their bow ties just right.

Boom Band Mac and Cheese

MACARONI AND CHEESE WITH TRUMPET PASTA

Butternut squash, peas, and yogurt make for a healthful mac and cheese. Cheddar keeps it deep, rich, and cheesy.

Kosher salt

12 ounces trumpet (campanelle) pasta

⅔ cup frozen peas

2 cups shredded extra-sharp cheddar

½ cup butternut squash purée (homemade, frozen, or canned)

½ cup plain whole-milk Greek yogurt

½ cup whole milk

⅛ teaspoon freshly grated nutmeg

2 tablespoons unsalted butter, cubed

1. Bring a large pot of heavily salted water to a boil. Cook the pasta according to the package directions, lowering in the peas 2 minutes before the pasta is al dente.

2. Meanwhile, stir together the cheese, squash, yogurt, milk, nutmeg, and ½ teaspoon salt.

3. Save 1 cup of the pasta water, then drain the pasta and peas. Return them to the pot over medium-low heat. Stir in the butter until melted. Fold in the squash mixture and stir until the cheese is melted and the sauce is smooth. If the sauce looks too thick, stir in some of the pasta water, a couple of tablespoons at a time.

4. Remove from the heat and serve immediately.

Say, what if a trumpet was made from a noodle?
I think it'd be fun if my pasta could tootle.
With butternut squash, and then yogurt and peas,
this mac and cheese marching band's certain to please!

TIME: 35 MINUTES, PLUS 8 HOURS RISING ✱ MAKES TWO 12-INCH PIZZAS, 4 TO 6 SERVINGS

If I Ran the Pizzeria

HOMEMADE DO-IT-YOUR-WAY PIZZAS

What if YOU ran the pizzeria? Well, now you do! Dream up your own toppings and then go shopping. Bring them home with your grown-up and get started chopping!

Extra-virgin olive oil
2 16-ounce balls of frozen pizza dough
1 14.5-ounce can of crushed tomatoes
Kosher salt
2 cups shredded mozzarella (8 ounces)
8 ounces fresh mozzarella, halved lengthwise and thinly sliced into half-moons

TOPPINGS THAT GO ON PIZZA BEFORE COOKING (CHOOSE AS MANY AS YOU LIKE):

Sliced mushrooms
Sliced black olives
Sliced green, yellow, or red bell peppers
Sliced pepperoni
Cooked and crumbled Italian sausage
Cooked ham
Blanched broccoli florets
Anchovies
Pineapple chunks

TOPPINGS THAT GO ON PIZZA AFTER COOKING:

Cooked bacon, roughly chopped
Baby spinach, torn
Shaved Parmesan
Flaky sea salt

1. Grease two medium bowls with a little oil, turn the pizza dough in the oil to coat, then cover with plastic wrap and let sit at room temperature until the dough thaws, puffs, and is no longer cold, about 8 hours.

2. An hour before you plan to bake, place a pizza stone or an upside-down baking sheet on the center rack of the oven. Heat the oven to 500°F.

3. Meanwhile, make the pizza sauce: In a blender, purée the crushed tomatoes, ¼ teaspoon salt, and a generous drizzle of oil until smooth.

4. Line a pizza peel or rimless cookie sheet with parchment paper. Stretch one of the dough balls into a 12-inch round, about ¼-inch thick, and place it on the parchment. Spread with about ¼ cup of the sauce, almost to the edge. Sprinkle with half of the cheese and your desired toppings. (Get creative as you design your pie!)

5. Slide the parchment paper with the pizza on it onto the preheated pizza stone or upside-down baking sheet and bake for 10 to 20 minutes, depending on how many toppings you have. You'll know it's ready when the cheese starts to brown on top and the crust has lots of golden spots underneath.

6. Use tongs to pull the hot pizza onto the peel or cookie sheet, then transfer it to a wire rack. Top with any additional toppings, if desired. Cool slightly, then serve. Repeat with the remaining dough and toppings.

They make a fine pizza
at most pizzerias.
But sausage and peppers?
They're average ideas.
If I made the pizza,
I'd change it, you see.
I'd dream up new toppings
for pies à la ME.

Fancy-Pants Lasagna

VEGETABLE LASAGNA WITH WALNUT "MEAT"

You'll go nuts for this meatless lasagna! The walnuts add tons of flavor and give it a chewier, chunkier, and, well . . . meatier texture than any vegetable lasagna you may have tried. It's fancy, but it's easy. There's nothing to fear.

15 ounces whole-milk ricotta

¼ cup grated Parmesan

¼ teaspoon freshly ground black pepper

Large pinch of freshly grated nutmeg

Kosher salt

1 10-ounce package of frozen spinach, thawed

1 14.5-ounce can of butternut squash or pumpkin purée

¼ cup whole milk

1 large egg

Nonstick cooking spray

1 24-ounce jar of tomato sauce

12 ounces no-boil lasagna noodles

½ cup finely chopped toasted walnuts (optional; see NOTE on page 76)

2 cups shredded mozzarella (8 ounces)

1. Heat the oven to 375°F. In a food processor or in a large bowl with a whisk, blend the ricotta, Parmesan, pepper, nutmeg, and ¼ teaspoon salt until smooth.

2. Use a clean kitchen towel to squeeze all the moisture from the thawed spinach. Use your fingers to break apart the spinach and add it to the food processor. Pulse a few times, until the spinach is chopped and combined. (If using a bowl, chop the spinach finely with a knife, then whisk it into the ricotta mixture.)

3. In a large bowl, whisk together the squash purée, milk, egg, and ½ teaspoon salt.

4. Coat a 9-inch square baking pan with nonstick cooking spray. Spread 3 tablespoons of tomato sauce evenly across the bottom. Cover with an even layer of lasagna noodles, then spread half of the ricotta mixture on top. Spread ¾ cup of tomato sauce over the ricotta, then top with another layer of noodles. Spread 1 cup of the butternut squash mixture over the noodles, then top with half of the walnuts, if using, and ¾ cup mozzarella.

A walnut lasagna?
It *frightens* me awfully.
Could I even cook it?
It *scares* the pants off me!
But it's easy to bake,
and when making lasagna,
your pants—even scaredy ones—
ought to stay on ya.

5. Repeat the layers, starting with the noodles, ricotta mixture, and tomato sauce, then the noodles, squash, walnuts, and mozzarella. Finish with a final layer of noodles, the remaining 1 cup tomato sauce, and the remaining mozzarella.

6. Cover with nonstick foil (or foil sprayed with nonstick cooking spray) and bake for 35 minutes. Remove the foil and bake until golden and bubbly, about another 20 minutes. Let cool at least 10 minutes before serving.

Who-Hash

SWEET POTATO, ONION, AND APPLE HASH

The sweetness of the sweet potato and apple in this dish will make even the tiniest heart grow three sizes. Hash is flexible by nature, so feel free to add other ingredients you may have in the kitchen. Make sure to cook it until crispy and browned at the edges. That's hash happiness!

1 pound sweet potato, coarsely grated (1 large or 2 medium potatoes)

1 yellow onion, coarsely grated

1 Granny Smith apple, coarsely grated

2 teaspoons kosher salt

Freshly ground black pepper

1 tablespoon extra-virgin olive oil, plus more as needed

1 tablespoon unsalted butter

Sour cream or plain Greek yogurt, for serving (optional)

Applesauce, for serving (optional)

1. In a bowl, combine the sweet potato, onion, and apple. Transfer the mixture to a clean kitchen towel and squeeze out the liquid over the sink. Keep squeezing until no more liquid comes out. Lots of squeezing = crispy hash. Put the mixture back into the bowl and stir in the salt, and pepper to taste.

2. Heat the oil and butter in a large nonstick skillet over medium-high heat. Add the potato mixture, patting it down into an even layer, and cook without disturbing for 3 to 5 minutes, until a crust develops on the bottom. Stir with a heatproof spatula, breaking up the crust, then cook undisturbed for another few minutes. (Add more oil if the pan looks dry.) Repeat a couple more times until browned and evenly crusted, then transfer to a serving platter. Top with sour cream or yogurt and applesauce, if you like, and serve.

What Cindy Lou *Who* has cooked up for the bash with apples and onions—it's scrumptious *Who-Hash!*
So this is the lesson from Cindy Lou's griddle:
A chef is a chef, no matter how little!

Roast Beast with Grinchy Citrus Sauce

ROAST BEEF WITH GARLIC AND HERBS AND ORANGE YOGURT SAUCE

Juicy roast beast—in this case, beef—gets a creamy, garlicky, citrusy sauce that's easy to whisk together while the roast is in the oven.

FOR THE ROAST BEAST:

- 4 garlic cloves, finely grated or minced
- 2 tablespoons minced fresh rosemary
- 1 teaspoon minced fresh thyme

  Large pinch of allspice

  Kosher salt and freshly ground black pepper

- 1 3-pound eye of round beef roast, tied with twine at 3-inch intervals
- 2 tablespoons extra-virgin olive oil

FOR THE GRINCHY CITRUS SAUCE:

- 1 cup plain whole-milk Greek yogurt
- 1 tablespoon freshly squeezed orange juice
- 1 teaspoon finely grated orange zest
- 1 garlic clove, finely grated or minced

  Kosher salt and freshly ground black pepper

1. MAKE THE ROAST BEAST: In a large bowl, stir together the garlic, rosemary, thyme, allspice, 1 tablespoon salt, and ½ teaspoon pepper. Rub this mixture all over the beef and let sit at room temperature for 1 hour.

2. Place a rack in the middle of the oven, and heat the oven to 350°F. Heat the oil in a large cast-iron skillet or other heavy ovenproof skillet over medium-high heat.

3. Put the beef in the skillet (reserving any herb rub in the bowl) and sear until well browned on all sides, about 3 minutes per side. Brush the reserved herb rub onto the beef, then transfer the skillet to the oven. How do you like

> The Whos lend a hand in the whole preparation—
> Who-cooking, you know, has a great reputation.
> They measure out orange juice, whisk up the yogurt.
> With beast sauce like this, not a bit gets leftover'd!

your roast beast cooked? For medium-rare, cook until the meat registers 125°F on an instant-read thermometer, about 50 minutes. (The beef will continue to cook a little after you remove it from the oven.) For medium, cook to 135°F, about 5 to 10 minutes longer.

4. Transfer the beef to a cutting board, tent loosely with foil, and let rest for 10 minutes.

5. MAKE THE GRINCHY CITRUS SAUCE: In a small bowl, whisk together the yogurt, orange juice, orange zest, garlic, and salt and pepper to taste.

6. Thinly slice the roast, and serve with the sauce on the side. When the Grinch hosts the holidays, who joins the feast?

I've come to your birthday to help you eat cake—
and as I'm well-known for the messes I make,
I have an idea to clean as I go:
by eating your cake in the bathtub, like so.

Cat in the Bath Birthday Cake

CHOCOLATE CAKE WITH STRAWBERRY MARSHMALLOWY FROSTING

This dark, moist chocolate cake is covered in swirls and swishes of strawberry marshmallow frosting—pink and just sweet enough. Wherever you decide to eat it, the frosting is guaranteed NOT to leave a ring.

FOR THE CAKE:

Nonstick cooking spray

2½ ounces bittersweet chocolate, chopped

1¼ cups hot decaffeinated coffee (or hot water)

2½ cups sugar

2 cups unsweetened Dutch-process cocoa powder

2¼ cups all-purpose flour

1½ teaspoons baking soda

1 teaspoon kosher salt

¾ teaspoon baking powder

1¼ cups buttermilk, or plain yogurt thinned with a little milk

⅔ cup neutral oil, such as grapeseed, sunflower, or canola

1 teaspoon vanilla extract

3 large eggs

FOR THE FROSTING:

8 ounces fresh strawberries, hulled

2 large egg whites

1½ cups sugar

Pinch of cream of tartar

Pinch of kosher salt

Sprinkles (optional)

1. MAKE THE CAKE: Heat the oven to 325°F. Spray three 9-inch cake pans with nonstick cooking spray and line the bottoms with parchment paper.

2. In a medium microwave-safe bowl, microwave the chocolate on medium-low power in 30-second intervals, stirring in between, until melted. Whisk in the coffee until completely combined, then set aside to cool.

3. In a large bowl, whisk together the sugar and cocoa powder until there are no lumps. Whisk in the flour, baking soda, salt, and baking powder.

4. In a separate bowl, whisk together the buttermilk, oil, and vanilla.

5. In another large bowl, beat the eggs with a handheld mixer until pale and frothy, about 3 minutes. Scrape in the

continues on next page

cooled chocolate mixture and beat to combine.

6. Pour in one-third of the buttermilk mixture and beat until just combined. Pour in one-third of the flour mixture and beat until just combined, then scrape down the sides of the bowl. Repeat two more times, alternating the buttermilk and flour mixtures, mixing just until the batter is smooth and free of lumps.

7. Divide the batter among the prepared pans and bake until the tops spring back when touched and a toothpick inserted in the center comes out clean, 30 to 35 minutes. Transfer the pans to a wire rack to cool completely.

8. When the cakes are cool, run a thin offset spatula or butter knife around the edges of the pans to loosen them, then invert them and remove the parchment paper. Turn the cakes right side up and trim the tops with a serrated knife so the layers are even.

9. When the cakes are trimmed, move on to the frosting. (Don't make the frosting ahead of time; it doesn't stay spreadable for very long. If needed, the cakes can be baked a day ahead and stored in the refrigerator tightly wrapped with plastic wrap.)

10. MAKE THE FROSTING: In a blender, purée the strawberries until very smooth, then press through a fine-mesh sieve. You should end up with ⅔ cup of strawberry purée.

11. Heat 1 inch of water in a medium pot until simmering.

12. In the metal bowl of a stand mixer, whisk together the strawberry purée, egg whites, sugar, cream of tartar, and salt. Place the bowl over the simmering water (without letting it touch the water) and whisk constantly until the sugar has dissolved (the bowl will heat up, so use an oven mitt to hold it). Transfer the bowl back to the mixer and whisk on high speed until thick and glossy with medium peaks, 3 to 5 minutes. (If you don't have a stand mixer, you can use a metal bowl and a handheld mixer or an immersion blender with a whisk attachment.) Use the frosting immediately.

13. Place one cake layer on a serving plate or cake stand and spread some of the frosting on top. Repeat with the remaining layers, stacking them on top of each other. Spread the frosting on the sides of the cake and smooth the top and sides, making swirls and swags if you like. Sprinkle with sprinkles, if using. This cake is best eaten the same day it's made.

Look what you cooked—
you must really be proud!
The food that you cooked
could delight a big crowd.

Since you cleaned as you went,
the last cleanup is less.
But giant or small,
have no fear of this mess!

Why so?
Turn the page for another
good trick that I know...

How to Clean Up
(A CAT IN THE HAT SPECIALTY)

The Cat in the Hat loves a good mess, but he's also a keen cleaner-upper. He always picks up his playthings, and the same goes for his Kitchen Things. If you do the same, your grown-up will always be pleased. And a spotless kitchen will be ready for your *next* cooking adventure.

CLEANUP CATLIST:

- Put away ingredients.
- Sort out compost, recycling, and trash.
- Wash the dishes or load the dishwasher.
- Wash and scour the pots and pans.
- Wipe down the countertops and stove.
- Sweep up the floor—and mop if needed.
- Store leftovers in containers.

**AND THAT,
SAYS THE CAT,
IS THAT.**

Because you wiped down and washed up as you went,
you've already made an astonishing dent.
The cleanup that's left will be done in a beat,
and then you can sit and get ready to eat!

Acknowledgments

For teaching me that wonderful things come from inspired messes, and for all the playful, rascally creatures who populate this book, I am warmly and forever grateful to Theodor Geisel, aka Dr. Seuss.

The recipes in this book were developed and delish-ified by Jade Zimmerman, who added zip and sparkle to every single one.

Christopher Testani's fabulous photos were perfectly adorned by Carla Gonzalez-Hart's playful props. The food you see was deliciously oomphed by stylist Barrett Washburne, and co-oomphed by Lauren Radel. Olivia Testani, along with Carla, were patient, graceful hand models and morsel tasters.

At Random House Children's Books, editors Alice Jonaitis and Jonathan Milder measured and tidied all the sentences, while copyediting by Barbara Perris, Stephanie Bay, Melinda Ackell, and Alison Kolani kept the words from going kablooey. Jenny Beal Davis designed a fun, fabulous world for it all, from foundations laid by Megan McLaughlin. Sonali Fry, Tracy Tyler, and Cathy Goldsmith at RHCB and Susan Brandt at Dr. Seuss Enterprises championed the book and helped make sure everything came out just right.

My agent, Janis Donnaud, agented till her agenter was sore. So, as the *Whos* say, I am "thankful and grateful to you!"

An extra-large bundle of thankage is due to the ones who helped out most: Melissa Clark, who showed me how to really have fun in the kitchen, and Dahlia Clark-Gercke, who is training me to be a good grown-up.

POP POP POP

Index

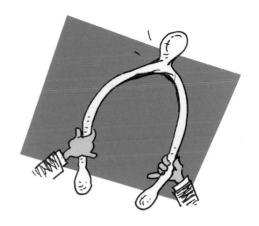

Daniel Gercke was born and raised in Colorado. This is his fifth cookbook, and though he has written cookbooks about pies, chickens, and zombies, at heart he has always been a Green Eggs and Ham kind of guy. His Bar-ba-loot suit still fits. He shares a very lively kitchen in Brooklyn, New York, with his wife, Melissa Clark, and their daughter, Dahlia.